M000166119

ENDORSEMENTS

"We're so grateful James took the time to pen this portion of his life's story, one filled with lessons learned from the trenches. May many be strengthened and encouraged so they too may be ambassadors of hope."

John and Lisa Bevere | messengerinternational.com

"Our friend James Goll has faced many challenges in recent years. We have watched him not only find hope but grow in faith, hope, and love in his arduous journey. May the lessons he has learned grip your heart and inspire you, so that you too can become a hero of hope in our generation."

Michael W. & Debbie Smith | michaelwsmith.com

"*Finding Hope* is raw and real life. It is a true life story of love and loss and regaining hope through it all. Navigating through such suffering and being willing to share with others is a great gift and James has done an excellent job. Thank you James for your transparency and for writing this book that will surely give great hope to others.

Bill & Beni Johnson | bjm.org and benij.org

"The life of our friend James Goll is a testimony of God's endless hope. With decades of experience in bringing hope to churches and individuals, James writes from a rich treasury of insight. *Finding Hope* is your opportunity to taste and see how good God's plan is for your life. Read it for the riches it contains, and let hope live again inside of your heart!"

Brian & Candice Simmons | thepassiontranslation.com

"Hard times will come to everyone, but few make it through tragedies with strength still in their step. Through real-life tales of resilience and key biblical insights, James Goll lights a beacon of hope that shines brightly with the testimony of Jesus Christ. Read and be encouraged—and just watch as that encouragement spreads to others!"

Dr. Ché & Sue Ahn | cheahn.org

"Do you need perspective on the trials of life and tools to help you to keep moving forward? I know this man and his life. The wisdom contained in this book will give you hope and will be a source of Good News to you."

Cindy Jacobs | generals.org

"In *Finding Hope* you will journey with James Goll as he surgically, with his words, opens his own heart to share with you the treasures of life he has gained. This is an essential legacy gift from a true father of the faith."

Mickey Robinson | mickeyrobinson.com

"In *Finding Hope*, James intentionally pushes past the boundaries of safe subjects and pat answers and reminds us that hope is both a disposition and a helmet. This book may be coming into your hands at the very moment you need to secure your helmet. You can trust James. I do."

Lance Wallnau | www.7mu.com

"Life can have many twists and turns. It's not how you start the race but how you finish. As you read this book, listen with your heart so you too can emerge from any fiery trials better than when you went in."

Harry R. Jackson Jr. | thehopeconnection.org

"In *Finding Hope*, James identifies heroes in his own walk through tremendous tragedy. However, I found myself thinking, *James Goll is my hero*. This book will provide you with the necessary guardrails for finding and staying connected to the goodness of God and a lifeline of hope."

Johnny and Elizabeth Enlow | johnnyandelizabeth.com

"I love James Goll. His life and courage are my best example of hope lived out. No one has the rich writing, communication skills, and understanding like James. This book must be read!"

Bob Hartley | bobhartley.org

"*Finding Hop*e shines a light through the darkness for those struggling through situations of loss, pain, confusion, and illness. James combines practical wisdom with his own moments of revelation as he passed through the valley of the shadow of death to produce the reality of overcoming faith. If you apply the lessons James learned, I believe you too will be numbered among those that overcame by the blood of the lamb and the word of their testimony."

Joan Hunter | joanhunter.org

FINDING
HOPE

*Rediscovering life
after Tragedy*

JAMES W. GOLL

BroadStreet
PUBLISHING

BroadStreet Publishing Group, LLC
Racine, Wisconsin, USA
www.broadstreetpublishing.com

FINDING HOPE
Rediscovering life After Tragedy

Copyright © 2015 James W. Goll

ISBN-13: 978-1-4245-5099-9 (hardcover)
ISBN-13: 978-1-4245-5100-2 (e-book)

Art direction by Tyler Goll (www.tylergoll.com)
Cover design by Chris Garborg (www.garborgdesignworks.com)
Interior by Katherine Lloyd (www.TheDESKonline.com)

Printed in China

8/15–1

DEDICATION

As you read this raw and transparent book, you will eventually come to the chapter entitled "Never, Never, Never Give Up!" For those of you who know my life, history, and stories, you already know what I am referring to. I will not spoil the story line of the roller-coaster ride contained in this book and the amazing statement concerning never quitting. But you will understand in due time.

With this backdrop, for what I think is my one last time of doing so, with all that is within me—I dedicate this book to my late wife, Michal Ann Goll, and to the ministry she founded, Compassion Acts, that we carry on in her honor to the nations to this day. She has been worshipping unabated in heaven now already for several years. You gave me hope. You never lost your smile. I am forever a better man because God sent this all-American girl into my life.

We will meet again at the waterside.

ACKNOWLEDGMENTS

Years ago I was taught to pray for three things on a regular basis: to ask God for the release of the fullness of the fruit of the Holy Spirit in order to have character to carry the gifts he gives; to pray for the fullness of the power of the Holy Spirit to release something that lasts beyond simply man's efforts; to pray for the wisdom ways of God in every facet of church and kingdom life.

Perhaps this book you hold in your hands goes more into this third category of prayer for the wisdom ways of God in every facet of life. I never dreamed I'd walk through the valley of the shadow of death. For me, Psalm 23 is a psalm for the living. The book of Psalms has been my guiding light for many years…and the book of Proverbs…and the book of John…and the book of…well, I'm sure you get the picture.

So I want to give credit to where credit is due—to all the writers of the sixty-six very diverse books of the Holy Bible. In doing so, I wish to honor God the Father, the Son, and the Holy Spirit—the Three in One.

The Bible has been my mainstay. And the ultimate Author of this unique Holy Book is the one who gives me life, hope, and resiliency to keep on bouncing back. Thank you, God, for the Bible.

CONTENTS

When I was ten years old I had a dream to become a rock star. In 1994 my dream had come true and in 2004 I was at the top of my professional career with millions of records sold. But I was completely empty; I was only a shell walking around with absolutely nothing meaningful inside. I was hooked on every drug you could think of. I was in total despair and nothing I had in the natural—and I had a lot—could help me out of my despair.

That's when everything changed.

A partner in real estate invited me to church where I heard about Jesus and how he'll come into your life and resurrect everything that is dead. I invited Jesus to come into my life and hope started to shine like a radiant light inside of me. I finally knew that I'd be able to eventually get out of the mess I was in.

After just a few weeks of praying, reading my Bible, going to church, and spending time talking with other Christians, I broke free from every addiction that held me captive, thanks to Jesus. I ended up leaving Korn and became a full-on follower of Jesus. It was beautiful in the beginning, but within three years I had lost everything. I had a net worth of about $10 million and had almost $3 million in cash when I left the band and started following Jesus. But I invested into a few bad business ideas and I ended up losing all of my money.

At one point things were so low that I made up a game with my six-year-old daughter of looking for change around the house so she could buy lunch the next day at school. I didn't know what I was going to do. I prayed and prayed and then finally one day a check came out of nowhere and landed in my mailbox at the perfect time. Financially, things started to shift for me right after that miracle check arrived. So yeah, I've had to find a lot of hope, even after meeting Jesus.

To me, hope is a deep inner-knowing that something good is right around the corner, even if you're in a pit of depression and you feel like you're lost. We all have to face things in life that are almost unbearable at times, which is why we need the foundation of hope inside of us.

That foundation of hope is knowing Jesus Christ, and Jesus is the resurrection and the life, so nothing can stay dead if we are in a relationship with him.

Nothing.

No matter how difficult or how dark—from the small set-backs, to the medium-size trials, to the horrific, horrendous trials, all the way to the day of our death—Jesus will resurrect everything and turn it around for good. This is the hope that must be anchored inside of our souls so we can get through anything that comes against us.

This hope is the truth and anything contrary is a lie.

I met James Goll in 2005. James is one of the most unique leaders I know. I just love his personality. His soul is a deep well. He is a theologian and a man of the Spirit, totally hungry after God. But on the other hand, he's one of the funniest guys I know as well—a great combination in my opinion!

When I heard about the trials his family was going through, I prayed a lot for him and tried to sow into his life however I could. When Michal Ann, the love of his life, passed away, my heart was so with him and his kids, but I just didn't know what to pray anymore. I was like, "God, I don't understand this. How can a person who's been so faithful to you encounter these trials that seem so overboard?"

To see how James and his family have come through these circumstances is mind-blowing. They've walked through some of the heaviest storms imaginable and their story has strengthened me even more to know that God truly does turn all things around for good.

We always need to have hope.

Always.

It must be a part of the foundation in our souls. When we feel negative circumstances weighing heavily upon us, deep down inside there's an ocean of peace that nothing can disturb because we know that we have that hope. Christ living inside of us is that hope, so it's impossible for hope to just disappear. Romans 8:28 is true: God will turn all things around for good for those who love him and are called to his good purpose.

It might take longer than we want, but God will always turn everything around for good if we'll trust and wait on him.

Finding Hope may be the most important book James Goll has ever written—and he has written a lot of books! You will definitely find hope in this book, so get ready to be strengthened and encouraged in a new way, and remember one thing...

Never.

Give.

Up.

Brian "Head" Welch
www.brianheadwelch.net

HAS TRAGEDY EVER STRUCK YOUR HOUSE?

did not pick this subject. In fact, I would never have picked it. If it had been up to me, I would have run a hundred miles in the opposite direction. But in the providence of God I think this topic has chosen me.

Finding Hope. If any of us is ever going to go looking for hope, there must be a reason for needing it. Most of the time, that reason involves tragedy—some hardship that is almost more than we can bear. So although I hope that tragedy has not struck your house, I suspect it must have if you have lived any length of time, and that, like me, you need to find hope too.

By "tragedy" I am not referring only to car accidents or natural disasters; rather, I am thinking of just about any kind of significant loss that can cause anguish to a person. You might term your own tragic events as calamities, misfortunes, catastrophes, heartbreaks, adversities, tribulations, distresses, hardships, privations, miseries, troubles, conflicts, griefs, sorrows, sufferings, pain, or just plain old hard times. Everybody is different, and what would seem like a tragedy to one person may seem easy for someone else.

Difficulty often strikes abruptly. You lose your job. Your friend rejects you. Your spouse dies (or even your beloved pet). You send off your precious son or daughter into military service in a war zone. Your church falls apart. You are served divorce papers. The economy nosedives and takes your savings right along with it. (How did the economic downturn of 2008 affect you? It created real tragedy for some of my friends.)

Tragedies reduce you to your elemental self. You feel weak. Temptations assail you, especially the temptation to despair. Joy vanishes, and the air around you seems heavy. "Woe" becomes part of your vocabulary, and the grass looks greener just about everywhere else except where you are now standing (or where you are curled up in the fetal position). You find it hard to get back up on your feet again every time you get knocked down, let alone to keep on walking forward.

Both Sides Now

"Both Sides Now" is the name of a folk song from the '60s, and it captures an important truth. I can now look at life from both sides, which I did not used to be able to do. I have experienced both heaven-sent highs and the bleakest lows—sometimes both of these in the same day. And, firsthand, I have learned some things about God that I did not used to know.

I have learned that it is OK to be real. Raw reality is better than any mask we could put on, especially the pat answers and the sugary smiles of religion (which ignore the fact that we may be bleeding to death inside).

I have learned to live life in the light of eternity, and I can identify with my namesake James, when he says that life is but a "vapor" (James 4:14, NKJV). That does not mean I am living some kind of pie-in-the-sky, everything's gonna be hunky-do-ry-bye-and-bye existence. It just means that I get it now. I get it. I know both sides of the stormy clouds now, and I know that my faithful, hope-imparting God holds me in his strong hands day and night. I have found that he is bigger than any tragedy I can cook up in my worst nightmare. He can handle anything, and joy truly *does* come in the morning (Psalm 30:5). Now I know, beyond a shadow of a doubt, that

> having been justified by faith, we have peace with God through our Lord Jesus Christ, through whom also we have access by faith into this grace in which we stand, and [we can] rejoice in hope of the glory of God. And not only that, but we also glory in tribulations, knowing that tribulation produces perseverance; and perseverance, character; and character, hope. Now hope does not disappoint, because the love of God has been poured out in our hearts by the Holy Spirit who was given to us. (Romans 5:1–5, NKJV)

I can look at the storm clouds from both sides now, and I can look at life from both sides of the pulpit. I have been a full-time vocational minister for over forty years. I have prayed for people; I have counseled people. I have learned many of the promises that are in the Bible, and I have tried to live up to its character values. But some things I never understood until I went through about twelve years of what could be considered trauma. My yardstick of judgment got tossed out the window. Now I understand some things about human frailty. I know what the driving force of pain can make me do, even though it does not give me a license to sin. I will never learn to enjoy having my life spiral out of control and I do not like pain any more than the next person—but now I appreciate what God can do with it.

In the pages that follow, allow me to give you a guided tour of my own triumph in the midst of tragedy. I hope to show you how to find hope for yourself. I promise to be real, because this is not going to touch your heart unless I share from mine.

Chapter One

WHEN THE BOTTOM FALLS OUT

Hope deferred makes the heart sick, but desire fulfilled is a tree of life.

—PROVERBS 13:12, NASB

was showering after working out at the YMCA one day when I noticed a little nodule. I thought, *Well, that's weird. Never noticed that before. What's that?* I wasn't exactly afraid, but it concerned me enough to make me go to the doctor. And that took me on a completely unexpected and unasked-for journey.

A stern oncologist did an initial bone marrow exam. The doctor's bedside manner did nothing to soften the impact of either the test or the results. I was so unprepared for this to be serious. They did not even take me to another room. They just brought this machine in and started the test. I am sure they anesthetized me, but frankly I have no recollection of the whole thing. I do remember being scantily clothed (which makes you feel even more vulnerable) and this machine making a buzzing noise. Next thing I know, I am being told that I have something called non-Hodgkin's lymphoma—cancer.

The Big C

I was battling the Big C. Or is it the little c? Yes, it has got to be the little c, because Christ is the Big C, and that proved to be the truth through seemingly endless rounds of treatments.

I remembered a dream I had earlier, and I realized that God had sent it to fortify me for what was about to happen. In the dream, enemies who seemed fierce and foreboding surrounded me. Then my perspective changed and I rose up so that I could look down on them. My paralyzing terror receded as I viewed these enemies, who now looked like little stick figures, from above. The voice of the Holy Spirit came to me in that dream: "And your enemies shall be like grasshoppers in your own sight," which echoes a verse from the book of Numbers in the Bible.

OK, but I still had to fight. Round one involved twenty-five radiation treatments, and they were not pleasant. In fact, it got pretty gruesome. At first the nodule grew so fast it was the size of a cluster of grapes, and the radiation treatments burned me badly.

I prayed, of course. And people around the world were praying for me too. I think I was at the point of about treatment number eighteen when I got prayed over at a gathering and it seemed like the authentic fire of God started flowing through my bloodstream. I had come in with the skin under my clothes blistered and broken, intensely painful and burned from the radiation. By the next morning when I got into the shower, I realized that I had received a miracle. The fiery presence of God had healed my burned skin. I had baby skin where the day before I had looked like a burn victim. I did not have to put special oils on anymore.

I went back to the radiologist, hoping that I wouldn't have to endure the next scheduled treatments, but they made me complete the whole regimen. It was so great to be healed. But the whole thing was like a roller-coaster ride. When it was over and I was declared cancer-free, we had a celebration in the Vanderbilt-Ingram Cancer Treatment Center. And even though we did not really have the money for it, I took my whole family on a cruise. I had my life back and my wife, Michal Ann, and I wanted to celebrate in a special way.

Who Turned Out the Lights?

After a couple of years, I went back to the doctor for a checkup. Unbelievably, the lymphoma had come back. Scans showed that it was now located in new places with some growths behind my stomach, which made radiation impossible. I started taking communion every day and doing everything I could to help fight this disease. I initiated all sorts of therapies—alternative, naturopathic, praying the Word, soaking in worship, and more. I got lots of prayer, but I was full of questions, and so were the people around me. Why me? What did I do wrong? I tried to figure out if I had opened the door to this somehow, but I really could not find anything. Seriously, how could this be happening to me? I'd had amazing encounters with God and he had healed me, hadn't he? All I could do was keep walking with God and my family, believing that these enemies would yet become like grasshoppers in my sight.

The growth behind my stomach grew some more and then just sort of paused. Then I found a goose egg emerging on my left shoulder. This second round of passive immunotherapy was even more intense than the first type of treatments, and my immune system was ravaged. All this was happening in the midst of a terrific amount of prayer from people who really know how to pray. But I was internally struggling. How could this be happening to me?

Round Three

Eventually, the growth on my shoulder disappeared, but the growth behind my stomach was just sitting there, rather large and looming. So I had half beaten cancer a second time.

Around Christmastime Michal Ann had severe pain followed by some tests that revealed seven bleeding polyps in her colon. They had to act quickly. She had cancer, too, and they put her in the hospital for major surgery. Now it was like the bottom of the boat had fallen out. Our four young adult kids (whom we always called our miracle kids, but that is another story) had *both* of their parents fighting cancer at the same time.

Michal Ann was plunged into a fight for her life, and she did a magnificent job. Everybody loved her because of her upbeat, positive personality. She was as genuine and unpretentious as they come, an all-American girl who, like me, grew up in rural Missouri. She had never let one negative word be around her, especially during this time. We were friends, we were lovers, and we were partners in ministry. Together, we had founded Ministry to the Nations and then Encounters Network. We had started Women on the Frontlines before she got sick, and then, even after her diagnosis, she launched Compassion Acts, a ministry that pulls together people and other ministries to bring hope to the poor and sick, to victims of political strife and natural disasters. As part of her work with Compassion Acts, she started going on mission trips to Pemba, Mozambique, to pray for people and to speak at the Iris Ministries school located there.

That is where she was when the bottom fell out of the bottom—I had to phone her to tell her the results of the test they had done just before she left. There she was, eight thousand miles from home, and this wonderfully positive, always-smiling wife of mine just lost it. What a dreadful phone call. I had to tell her that the cancer had reexploded in her liver, which was a death sentence. By that time she had already had three organs cut out of her body and she had an ostomy bag, but she thought she had beaten the little c.

I remember being on that international phone call with her for twenty minutes, and she just sobbed the whole time. Seriously, I do not know which is more painful, the physical pain of the cancer itself or the loss of hope. We had to say good-bye on the phone and we knew we were going to have to say good-bye to life as we had known it. It was one of the worst days of married life we had ever experienced.

The Loss of My Companion

I will never forget the date in 2008—September 15. Momen-tously, that is the very date the United States economy tanked. I remember thinking, *A lady knows when to leave.* I will tell you the rest of that story later in this book. Except for that time on the phone, my Annie never surrendered her positive attitude. She never, ever complained. She always kept her smile.

After the dire diagnosis, four years passed, filled with ups and downs and pain. Then I lost her, the only woman I have ever loved, the only woman I have ever been with. We were married for thirty-two and a half years and we had delighted in our four children, traveled the globe, and written books together. We had prayed together daily and we knew the true meaning of the word *love.* We had battled our cancers together, too, and together we had undertaken every treatment available. But still, I lost my wife.

The love of my life had passed away. Her body was lowered into the ground in beautiful Dover cemetery in Missouri, right next to her parents. Her spirit is doing quite well, I know, but as the one left behind I did not think my pain would ever end.

I am no good with Band-Aids. Some people say I live with my feelings on my sleeve. I am a passionate person, and I live from my heart, which means my joy can be great, but my pain tears me to pieces. It has not been at all easy to get through this, even sometimes now.

Me, a widower? Me, a single parent? I never, ever thought that could happen. Me, in debt? Me, the guy who had never missed one payment in my entire life on anything? I was drowning in $300,000 of medical debt.

Living near Nashville, it was as if I was singing one of those mournful country songs: "My wife left me...my money's all gone...my dog died..." (By the way, my dog did die after Michal Ann, too, after fourteen years of sleeping in our bedroom every night.) Where was the so-called "abundant life" that Jesus talked about (John 10:10)?

The Goldfish Bowl

The life I was living I did not want and I would not wish on anybody else. All I could feel was pain and sorrow and anguish and grief. I hear there are five steps to recover from grief. I think I tried to skip over a couple of them.

Part of my problem was that I was also a public person, and I was living in a public "goldfish bowl" with my children. I had chosen that lifestyle, but my kids had not. None of them had ever volunteered to submit themselves to so much public scrutiny and unsolicited advice. For the most part, people were well meaning, but nobody likes to have their weaknesses and dilemmas exposed and "fixed."

It was as though Job's friends came out of the woodwork wherever I went; people gave me so many different interpretations of where I had gone wrong and what I should do now. I used to say I could find nothing useful in two books of the Bible: Leviticus and Job. Now I felt like Job was my personal friend.

I continued in public ministry. I had to. I had no other means of earning a living. I would go places and preach with my heart either just absolutely dead or hemorrhaging with pain and loneliness. As well as I could, I was trying to be faithful and prayerful, to offer up a "sacrifice of praise." I was fragile, and a lot of people lost patience with me. Thankfully, some did not.

Still, I lost 70 percent of the financial contributors who had taken years to pull together. I think some people just thought, *Well, it has to be sin because his wife died and he has fought off cancer at least twice.* Maybe some did not want to be associated to someone who was going through such a severe level of attack and calamity. I do not expect to understand what happened with the people who had once stood with me. But I have learned to bless any and all!

I Have *What?* Again?

In 2009, a year after Michal Ann graduated to heaven, I found out that my cancer had returned—this time with a vengeance. The growth behind my stomach had grown to the size of a large baked potato and the cancer had reached around to the front of my stomach and started going down my right leg. I hardly dared to tell anybody about the extent of it. People had their own lives to live, and surely they were getting tired of hearing from the one some considered "the boy who cried wolf," let alone rallying around me.

Would this affliction ever, ever end? I was still getting prayer. I still believed God. I was still doing everything I knew how to do to get better and stay healthy. But I had to find something I did not even realize I had lost—my helmet. Huh? Yes, in the midst of the battle for my life, I had mislaid my helmet of the hope of salvation (1 Thessalonians 5:8).

Ephesians 6 talks about putting on the whole armor of God, and the helmet is one of the most important pieces of protection. I had to make sure that my helmet was positioned firmly on my head, because most of this battle was taking place in my thoughts, in my mind. If I wanted to turn the tide of the battle, I was going to have to get my hope back.

What is hope? According to Mr. Webster, it means to cherish a desire with an expectation of fulfillment. Hope is a confident anticipation of good. It is not just wishful thinking or thinking positive. It is *not* the same as saying, "Well, I hope so." Hope is as solid as a helmet, but no helmet will protect you from danger if you have laid it aside.

Although my world had crashed in around me, I needed to be able to say to myself, "Something good is about to happen." I sure did not feel like it. I felt abandoned, and I did not know at all how I was going to make it. I hardly knew where to begin speaking to my own thoughts and emotions or how to graft the Word of Life inside myself. I was going to have to reach deep into God's resources, because I did not have any reserves left within me to keep me moving forward. I didn't even have much hope anymore, because it seemed to have been crushed so many times.

Hope Deferred

I started this chapter with the following verse from the book of Proverbs: "Hope deferred makes the heart sick, but desire fulfilled is a tree of life" (Proverbs 13:12, NASB). Hope deferred means hope postponed or delayed. That means that something you were expecting to happen did not happen—or it did not happen as you thought it would—and that not only makes the heart sick, but often the body and mind too. Hope deferred means more than waiting an extra day for a Christmas present. Hope is a heart thing, a life-giving thing, and when it falters or sputters out, we stumble, sometimes badly, often feeling as if we might be the only one on the planet going through such a thing.

Naturally, we can't wait to get to the second part of the proverb: "desire fulfilled is a tree of life." But we always need to start our journey in the first half of the verse.

Battle of the Heart

The whole thing is a heart battle. Here is another proverb about that: "Watch over your heart with all diligence, for from it flow the springs of life" (Proverbs 4:23, NASB).

How does it work? If you do a quick study of the "heart"

Scriptures, you will find that you can have a dull heart and a slow heart. You can have a hard heart, but you can also have a sensitive, tender heart. Your heart can make you vibrant and vigorous—or robotic and plodding. In order to understand your heart, you do not need to study cardiology. You do, however, need to learn how your spirit operates. I have learned that the only way that I can enjoy life and enjoy God and enjoy the people around me in the present tense is by keeping my heart pumping—even when it hurts to do so.

There are three typical responses to pain or rejection that deaden our hearts:

1. We move away from people and God.
2. We move toward some other source of relief or acceptance.
3. We move against others.

I have tried all three ways, and I do not recommend any of them. I have moved away from others and isolated myself. Some people move away from church or family as well.

I have moved toward seeming sources of acceptance, sometimes pretty aggressively—forgetting that God's acceptance is all that I need. We all know people in pain who have moved from place to place, even spouse to spouse, looking for fulfillment in all the wrong places. (We have such a need to be accepted, to be known and appreciated, so we do whatever we feel we need to do to get approval from others.)

Then there is bitterness, with which we move against

others. The pain settles deeper, and now, in addition to isolating ourselves and trying to find acceptance in some "safe" place, we develop judgments against the ones we see as perpetrators of our pain. We move against the community of believers and our families. We may even move against God. We get adversarial and then shift over into a victim mindset. Our glass is perpetually half empty and no one had better contradict our opinion on that score.

What Are My Core Values?

In order to learn to hope again, I had to go back to my ABCs, to my foundations. What did it matter that I was a professional minister who had traveled the globe and ministered in over fifty nations and had written over thirty books? I had to start back at the bottom.

I figured out three core values: (1) God is good all the time; (2) "all things work together for good to those who love God, to those who are the called according to His purpose" (Romans 8:28, NKJV); and (3) something good is just about to happen.

Number one, "God is good all the time" is not just a catchphrase. I read the Bible from front to back all over again and it convinced me that God just *does not* make mistakes. He loves me. In fact, he loves everybody. He knows what he is doing. We just have to believe that, even when we are feeling as if the very life has been snuffed out of us.

"All things work together for good..." That scriptural

advice has too often been used glibly by people who feel they must say something helpful in the face of tragedy. But the fact that it has been overused does not invalidate it! This is not to say that everything that happens *is* good. But if you continue to walk with God, he will take your broken pieces and supernaturally mend them, and that is an absolute miracle. With him, hope is on the way.

"Something good is just about to happen." That one seems to follow logically from the other two. How in the world can so much tragedy work out for good? I do not know, but God does. Who can bring light to this dark night of the soul? Only he can.

Hero of Hope—Job

At the end of each chapter I will be sharing a short story of someone I feel personifies the theme of that chapter. I hope they encourage you as they have me, and I highly encourage you to read more about these amazing heroes of hope.

The book of Job tells the story of a man who had amazing tenacity. He kept walking in his integrity even when he lost everything and everybody. Controversy swirled around him, and his wife and friends gave him terrible advice, but he still endured. It takes a hero to do that. He didn't really understand God's character until later, but he kept believing in him.

At the end of Job's story, there is a pivot point that takes place. His patience and perseverance (held up in James 5:11 as heroic) gets rewarded. Instead of disputing with his friends, he prays for them (Job 42:8, 10). And then good things began to happen again. The end of Job's life was much better than the beginning, because the Lord gave him twice as much as he had before, and a very long life in which to enjoy it.

Like Job, I had to learn to "redemptively interpret" all the people who wanted to fix me. When I did that, I realized that they just wanted me to be well. They were trying their best to help me get well because they actually cared about me. So instead of resisting them on the grounds of the fact that they could not understand my incomprehensible losses, I began to pray for them and bless them.

So if the bottom has fallen out for you, take a moment to pray with me right now as we begin to rediscover life together.

Prayer

Father, I present myself to you in Jesus' great name, and I declare that you are the source of my life. In you I live and breathe and have my very being. Take me on a journey to a place where hope is no longer deferred but where fulfilled desire becomes a tree of life. As I come running into your arms of redemptive love, do what only you can do. Only in you can all things be made new. Amen.

Finding Hope Takeaways

Chapter 1
When the Bottom Falls Out

✦ Hope is a confident anticipation of good. Tragedies deprive you of good things and take away your hope.

✦ Hope is vital to your well-being. How can you start to find it again?

  • Evaluate your responses to your pain. Get help to find your way past automatic reactions such as bitterness and despair.

  • Figure out the core values of your life.

  • Put on your "helmet of the hope of salvation" (1 Thessalonians 5:8), which protects your soul and spirit.

Chapter Two

ANYBODY GOT
A ROAD MAP?

*"For I know the plans that I have for you," declares
the LORD, "plans for welfare and not for calamity
to give you a future and a hope."*

—JEREMIAH 29:11, NASB

H ere I was, the guy who used to write books that would explain three hundred Scripture verses, and I could not figure out what to do in the short term, let alone the long term. I had lost so much—so many relationships and ministry connections, so much income, even so much sleep—I could hardly keep track of what day of the week it was. It did not take me long to recognize the fact that, before all of this happened, I used to take too much for granted, such as my health and basic contentment. But that realization was not very useful in the present moment when it came to getting through one day after another, and especially through the nights. (The nights were the worst.) My resilience was depleted and my gifts and credentials did not seem to matter much anymore. I was groping in the dark.

It is impossible to travel safely in pitch-blackness unless you have some kind of navigation system. Even if you are not particularly directionally challenged, as I happen to be—I can get lost even on my way to the airport—you can't stay on any road or path in the dark. You need guidance, some kind of GPS (Global Positioning System) to take over. When you are going through a dark night of the soul for whatever reason, it may take a while before you remember that God is your GPS—and that he wants you to have his help.

Has this been your experience? Or do you know in theory that he is your GPS, but you wonder if he knows your name and address anymore? When you go through severe stress, you tend to lose your bearings. You might have always walked with God, but now you barely recall what those days were like. You used to be able to follow his directions, but now your road map is lying crumpled in the dirt and everything around you looks unfamiliar. You feel absolutely lost.

To find your way again, you are going to need directions that are super simple and easy to follow. I did not remember that at first. As I mentioned in the previous chapter, I had to go back and rediscover my core values because it seemed that was all I had left. I also decided to lay hold of the "main and plain" doctrines of the faith, and to stick with the Word of God. I reviewed the facts: Jesus Christ is the only Son of God. Salvation comes by grace through faith in him. My life matters to him. There is an eternity and a heaven. God's Word has authority. Et cetera.

But did God really care about me? The minute I allowed myself to wonder if maybe I was an exception to God's Word, I began to flounder again. The enemy takes advantage of our doubts. *Did God really say that? Is anything an absolute truth?* I would think to myself. Down I would go. *Well, maybe God does love people in general, but I'm so far from him, I don't think he loves me anymore. I am just another number.*

I found out that I could not even rely on my memory of what God is like. I had to review the written Word often. God's Word is the complete road map for yesterday, today, and tomorrow. But you have to *look* at the map, right now. It is not good enough to have looked at it five or ten years ago. I had to reexamine what it says—each day. I had to stick to it and follow its directions.

Once again, the Word of God proved to be a lifeline for my soul. I rediscovered that it could show me the way through any wilderness or wasteland I found myself in.

Run to God!

As I kept reading the Word, I ran across what the disciples had said to Jesus: "Lord, to whom shall we go? You have words of eternal life" (John 6:68, NASB). They did not have anywhere else to turn, and neither did I.

What makes us think that our pain will go away if we run *away* from God? He is our Redeemer. He redeems our lives from destruction (Psalm 103:4)! He gives us a redemptive understanding of our circumstances.

Are you lost and miserable? Abandon yourself to him. Run straight into his arms. He will speak the words of life to you. He is your refuge. He is your stronghold of hope. He is always there for you; all you have to do is turn to him and say, "Here I am."

Make sure you turn to him and not to somebody else or to something that can medicate your pain. In times of trouble, establish some firm boundaries for yourself. God will never leave you, but you can turn away from him, repeatedly. In your distress and disillusionment, you can resort to old addictions or unhealthy patterns. Lots of times, people go back to the sources of comfort they knew before they came to Christ. They opt for alcohol, drugs, illicit relationships, pornography, or gambling. They fall back into gossip, blame, shame, strongholds of poverty, or defensiveness. It will be different for every person.

Some people isolate themselves. Others feel they have just got to be around other people all of the time. They're just trying to lessen the pain somehow, but it means that they are wandering around in the dark until they realize that the need to set their minds and hearts on God alone. Figure out what your personal default setting is, and do whatever you need to do to avoid it.

It is no use chafing about the situation. Hard stuff happens, and most of it seems unjust and unwarranted. But God is still good and he is still there for you. As one of my fathers in the faith told me, "The book of Job is still in the Bible." God has never changed the way life works. What the devil meant for evil, God will always turn around for good.

What has this got to do with finding hope and rediscovering life after tragedy? A whole lot, because you can make things much worse than you need to. You will find hope more quickly if you partner with God in the midst of your pain.

Run to a Trusted Community

One of the places God's road map will take you is to people you can trust—people who love well. Most of the time, this will include your family. For me it did. I ran to my kids, who were young adults. "You ran to your *kids?*" you may say. "You are their father!" Well, I tried to lean on them, and I know that sometimes I was a little too much for them. But even though their mother was gone, we were still family, and forgiveness covers a lot of fumbling around. In my case, four kids soon became eight, because all four of them got married within a three-year span, and now they are having kids of their own, so I am a grandpa. I will never be a perfect father, but I love my kids like crazy (I talk about them all the time), and they love me back. And we have learned to fight together to maintain a semblance of something called family.

I also ran to my friends. What a gift they are! I owe a lot to Bill Greenman, vice president of my board of directors. That man has a gift of faith. I remember one time I needed a friend with me at one of those intense oncology appointments, and he was there for me. And when I had to have serious back surgery in June of 2014 (which I haven't told you about yet), he and a few other trusted friends were the ones who chauffeured me around for more than four and a half months when I could not drive.

I am so thankful my dear friend Mickey Robinson, who has a strong gift of encouragement, like Barnabas. He survived a plane crash many years ago, and the strength he received from God and others he now shares with his friends. He checks in on me, and I appreciate him so much. He is the brother I never had.

You do not have to have dozens of friends when you have a few really good ones. In fact, four will be enough to carry your cot and to help get you into the presence of Jesus (Mark 2:4; Luke 5:19). At some point in time, you will need to be one of the four carriers yourself, and then at other times you will need their help.

Run to people who love you and who are able to bring you into the presence of the Lord. I have been blessed to have the counsel of those who are older and wiser in the faith, such as "Papa" Don Finto, who is now in his mid-eighties. That man loves the hell out of people, and that is a direct quote. I wish everybody could have someone like him to talk to when they are going through hard times.

You may be saying, "Well, that's nice for you, James, but I don't have anybody like that." I would say back to you, "You have the greatest friend in the world, and he is right with you day and night." Ask him to come to you. I had a period of about a month when the Holy Spirit would wake me up in the morning with a different secular song. One morning, for example, it was James Taylor's song, "You've Got a Friend," which says that when nothing's going right and you are down and troubled needing a helping hand, you have a friend. I knew who my friend was! Someone to help me "climb every mountain"!

Maybe it is true that you do not have family to run to and your trust has been eroded because even your friends (much like Job's) have turned on you. But even if you have good people in your life as I do, they cannot really meet your deepest needs anyway. My kids could not meet my needs, and I had to come to grips with the reality that I could not meet theirs. At the end of the day, friends can never meet your needs. Just remember to call out the name of Jesus, and the greatest brother and friend of them all will come to you. He believes in you and he knows what to do.

Worship God with Your Questions

You do not have to call out to Jesus in a prescribed way, using special religious language. You certainly do not have to have yourself figured out beforehand. When you call out to Jesus, you can bring anything to him, even your unresolved questions. Those unresolved questions can actually be a form of actual worship.

Worship God with your *questions*? You would want your questions answered, wouldn't you? Yes, but I have discovered that one of the best ways to get them answered (and quickly) is to entrust them to him in worship. Worship him by trusting him with your biggest, messiest questions. Tell him you do not know the answers, but you know he does and you will wait in full expectation for something good to come. He wants you to do this, whether you bring him some big philosophical or religious question, or (more than likely) some emotion-laden practical thing.

For example, my wife had some horses and somebody needed to keep taking care of them after she died. My youngest son went down to the barn and fed the horses every day for the whole first year, when I just could not go down there. That barn represented so much pain for me, because it was a place Michal Ann Goll loved. I hated that barn because she had loved it so much.

Then the time came when I just had to get over it. I went down there for about an hour, hay allergies and all. I fed the horses. My eyes watered and my nose ran and I hated every minute of it. I went again and it did not get any easier. I remember the day I went to the barn and I crawled up into the loft that was full of hay. I could not stand it. I opened the hayloft doors and I just started screaming. I wept a whole lot. I needed to "let it out" and express my feelings, and I decided that God was safe enough to take it. I found out that he was not the least bit offended when I told him how much I hurt and could not stand that barn.

I don't remember what I screamed, but I can tell you that it was not "I hate you" or anything like that. I just screamed my pain. And guess what? My scream of pain turned into praise. I started thanking God for those horses and for that barn. I started thanking God for that stinking hay. I did not understand it all, but when I turned all of my unanswered questions into praise, I began to offer a true sacrifice of praise.

True worship comes from the heart. I learned how to take care of the barn and the horses. (I tried, anyway.) And I learned to love that place. Enjoy it, even. It became a place of healing for me. Worshiping in one of the places of my greatest pain enabled me to trust him with all my heart. Oh, the agony and the ecstasy!

Trust is a form of understanding. Trusting means not leaning on my own understanding, but rather on his (Proverbs 3:5–6). And out of that comes hope and a certain amount of joy. I might never understand the answers to all my questions on this side of heaven, but one day I will. The reality is that, right now, we all see through a mirror dimly (1 Corinthians 13:12), and sometimes the only way to worship is to worship God with our questions.

The Importance of Forgiveness

Along with "being real" with my painful, unresolved questions and working them through with God's help, I had to forgive a lot.

I cannot overstate the importance of forgiveness, which is a prominent part of Jesus's message. I mentioned feeling as though I were surrounded by Job's friends, as people pressed in with their unwelcome advice. Would it have helped to express my exasperation to them and to drive them away? Was that what Job did? Well, no. With God's help, Job prayed for his friends (Job 42:8, 10). He blessed them even though he had not experienced much blessing from their interference. In a similar way, I took it upon myself to forgive the "Job's comforters" around me for their heavy-handed efforts, and I blessed them. Repeatedly. I released them from my judgment. I allowed gratitude to take over.

On top of that, I had to forgive myself for the self-imposed expectations that I had not met. That may sound a little crazy, but it worked. I had taken a beating and I had fallen for too many discouraging lies about myself. As a result, I found myself in sort of a cul-de-sac, going nowhere. In forgiving myself, I let him be my Savior once again. Forgiveness was like putting the key into the ignition of my stalled life.

Forgiveness is a choice. I did not have to *like* what had happened. I just had to forgive myself and others, and then I could turn around. I could turn back to God and then he could minister new life to me.

Nobody could do it for me, and I couldn't do it for anybody else, including my kids. I just had to turn away from the gripy "woe is me" attitude and affirm that God is the source of my life. Yes, in him I live and move and have my being (Acts 17:28). I told him that I would follow him wherever he took me. I remembered that Jesus's disciples had to make that decision, too, and that he had led them into some pretty intense stuff. I wanted to follow him, even if it meant more pain. I never wanted to hear my Lord say, "You do not want to go away also, do you?" (John 6:67, NASB).

Somehow—and I do not think any of us understands quite

how this works—practicing forgiveness leads directly to a restoration of hope. Fact stated. Period!

Pictures of Hope

In the book of Hebrews we find hope pictured in two ways, as a place of refuge and as an anchor:

> Therefore, we who have fled to him for refuge can have great confidence as we hold to the hope that lies before us. This hope is a strong and trustworthy anchor for our souls. It leads us through the curtain into God's inner sanctuary. Jesus has already gone in there for us. He has become our eternal High Priest in the order of Melchizedek. (Hebrews 6:17–20, NLT)

We can hold onto hope as the fugitives used to hang onto the horns of the altar in the ancient Israelite cities of refuge (Numbers 35). In those days, if someone sinned in a way that made him liable to punishment under the law, he could run to a designated city of refuge and be safe. God is our city of refuge; when we run to him we can grab hold of hope.

Hope will secure our emotions, which crash like wild waves inside our souls and threaten to drown us. Hope is the strong and trustworthy anchor for our souls. In an unstable, impermanent, ever-changing world, hope fastens us to the bedrock of God, the Rock of Ages. Within the sanctuary of God, anchored firmly on him, we are safer than ever—safer, believe it or not, than before the storm engulfed us.

Heroine of Hope—Rebecca Springer

I am building my own hall of heroes, something like the list of saints in Hebrews 11 (the "faith hall of fame"). Putting this together is part of my journey, and I want to share with you what I have discovered. Besides Job, I discovered another hero, a woman named Rebecca Springer. She lived from 1832 to 1904, and she wrote a Christian book called *Intra Muros* (Latin for *Within the Walls*), which has been revised and published under slightly different titles over the years. The version I have is called *Within Heaven's Gates,* and my eldest son gave it to me in hopes of providing me some help and perspective. I liked it so much I gave copies of this amazing book to all four of my kids the first Christmas after Michal Ann's death.

Rebecca Springer was the daughter of a Methodist clergyman and she attended Wesleyan Female College, graduating at eighteen. Then she married William, a lawyer who was a member of the Illinois General Assembly. At one point in her life, Rebecca was in failing health herself, and she almost died. Instead of dying, however, God took her on an extended journey to heaven, which she recorded in this book.

In her accounts, she tells about a riverside where you can go and meet loved ones who have preceded you to heaven. For a person who has lost someone precious, it is profoundly hope building to hear about how we are going to be separated only for a while. And it is so good to realize that since we will one day meet on the other side, we should continue to live a full life here. My youngest daughter was so moved by reading this account that she composed a touching song about this reality and recorded it with her producer husband. The transparent song is aptly called "Waterside," and is one of the most impacting tracks from their August York recording. Yes, we might feel as if we are swimming upstream and just trying to keep our heads above water when the bottom falls out. But there is a day that we will meet again at the shore on the other side.

Rebecca Springer is a heroine of hope to me because she gives me an eternal perspective on the losses I have suffered already, as well as on those yet to come. I do not expect to duplicate her experience of visiting heaven while I am still alive, but reading about her experience gives me a very real road map to follow—because, as we know, the narrow and winding road to heaven starts right here on earth, and it can be all too easy to wander from it.

Prayer

Father, instead of masking my pain, I bring it to you. I choose to worship you with my questions. I believe that Jesus came to heal the brokenhearted and to set at liberty those who are oppressed. I present my past, my present, and all that I hope to be—my future—to you. I choose to believe that you have a hope-filled plan for the rest of my life. Gracious Lord Jesus, thank you! Amen.

Finding Hope Takeaways

✦ God is the only one who can help you navigate your dark journey—and he wants to help you.

✦ How can you find the hope that is both a place of refuge and an anchor (Hebrews 6:17–20)?

- Run to God, and run to trusted people.

- Worship God with your unanswered questions.

- Forgive.

Chapter Three

CATCHING THE LITTLE FOXES

> *Great is Your faithfulness.* "*The* LORD *is my portion*," *says my soul,* "*Therefore I hope in Him!*"
>
> —LAMENTATIONS 3:23–24, NKJV

One bleak day, my EQ (Emotional Quotient) was at rock bottom. I do not remember how many of my kids were home that day, but I felt so overwhelmed that I retreated to the privacy of my bedroom and began to sob uncontrollably. Before long, weeping even harder, I went into my bathroom and shut the door. What I really wanted to do was to crawl into a hole in the ground and never come out, but that was impossible. So to put as much distance between myself and my painful situation as I could, I went through the only remaining door, which led to my walk-in closet.

With three doors between me and the rest of the house, I thought maybe I could hide from not only my family but also from God. But thanks to my oldest daughter, whose bedroom was on the second floor right above me, I was not allowed to self-destruct for long. I wish everyone could have someone like this tenacious young adult of mine, someone who can "get in your face" with tough love.

Thinking I had isolated myself completely, I was startled to hear a little knock on the door of the closet. "Dad?" The light switched on as she let herself in. "Dad, you seem to think we are the only family going through tragedy, but we are not. Everybody goes through difficulty at some point in life."

One moment I was beside myself with hopeless grief and the next moment I was confronted with reality by someone who cared enough to seek me out. What's more, this someone was not afraid to break up my pity party and tell me what to do. Next, I heard, "You think that we are elite and that we're above this, but we are not. You just have to get over this!"

Stop the World—I Want to Get Off!

Not that it was easy to get over this. I just wanted it to stop. Many days, I did not want to even get out of bed in the morning. I just wanted to pull the covers up over my head and pretend that nothing had happened. Of course that is called "denial," and it is not as safe as it would seem in there under the covers. What was it that Jesus said—"You will know the truth, and the truth will set you free" (John 8:32, NIV)? *Truth,* not denial, would set me free.

For the first year after Michal Ann graduated to heaven, I kept a private journal called "Dear Annie" so that I could keep processing my emotions and sorting out the situation with as much of God's light as I could manage. One day, I wrote, "Could we just stop the world from spinning today? I am not quite sure how much more of this spin I can take. Stop the world—I want to get off!" I was spiraling downward into thought patterns that I never dreamed I would get into. I had been walking with my best friend, Jesus, since I was three years old, but now I felt I was losing touch with him. I knew this happened to other people, but I never expected it to happen to me. I *knew* the truth! Or did I? I began to turn over every stone in my mind.

As may always be the case, it was the little issues that added up and attempted to pull me under. Emotionally, I was so close to the tipping point that I would be crushed by small slights and disappointments that would never have bothered me otherwise. I felt like a pot of simmering water on the stove that had been heated to almost the boiling point; all it took was one little thing more and I would spill over. Everything came into play: my particular mix of gifts and sensitivities, my background and experiences, the culture I grew up with, even my birth order.

All of us are different, but we all have a tipping (or boiling) point. What we do not know about ourselves can hurt us—and others as well. It takes hard experience to learn how to turn down the heat in the midst of our distress.

One Thought Leads to the Next

The reason behind the title of this chapter, "Catching the Little Foxes," has to do with the sneaky way little harmless issues can accumulate and bring you down. It comes from a line in the

Song of Solomon: "Catch us the foxes, the little foxes that spoil the vines, for our vines have tender grapes" (Song of Solomon 2:15, NKJV). We need to capture those foxlike little thoughts before they ruin everything we have worked so hard to cultivate.

The first little fox tiptoes into your troubled mind and makes you think, *I feel so alone.* Then, all of the sudden, we think, *Worse, I feel cut off. In fact, I feel utterly rejected. I'm just a piece of discarded trash as far as everyone, including God, is concerned. I don't think there's a place for me in the body of Christ. My future is ruined.*

You know who sends these foxes, don't you? The devil himself, the one who is skilled at wrapping the truth in a lie. Yes, you feel alone. But after you give in to that sad truth, the lies start to roll in. Cut off? Rejected? Discarded trash? That is false! The only one it holds true for is, in fact, the devil himself. He's the one who has been cut off and rejected, not you. He just wants your company, and he does *not* wish you well. The devil is the one who has no future in the body of Christ, not you. He is the hopeless one, not you, and he is attempting to lure you into his lair so he can eat you for lunch. Resist him!

> Stay alert! Watch out for your great enemy, the devil. He prowls around like a roaring lion, looking for someone to devour. Stand firm against him, and be strong in your faith. Remember that your family of believers all over the world is going through the same kind of suffering you are. (1 Peter 5:8–9, NLT)

One of his oldest tricks is to speak in the first person. He plants those thoughts in your mind, and you think they are truly your own. *I feel so bad today. It's downhill from here. I'm never going to be happy again.* You swallow these lines, because they seem to apply so accurately to your situation. It does not occur to you to counter them with scriptural truth. You are thinking, *I feel so cut off from God.* But if you are in Christ Jesus, you are not cut off—you have been grafted into the family of God with full access to the throne of grace to receive help and mercy in your time of need (Hebrews 4:16).

You do not have to stay where you are. Just because you got lured into a downward spiral of thinking does not mean you have to stay down there. Even though you may carry some unhealed hurts from the past or some unforgiveness, that should not relegate you to a condition of hopelessness. What went spiraling downward *can* be turned around. You can spiral up too. You can take one step after another onto a succession of truths until you come back up to where you can breathe God's pure air again. Yes, you can! All things are possible.

Romans 12:2 urges us to *renew* our minds. With the help of the Holy Spirit, your thinking can be transformed so that you can "prove what is that good and acceptable and perfect will of God" (NKJV). If you are able to *prove* something, then it must be true. What *is* that good and acceptable and perfect will of God? That must be something worth hoping for. The specifics will vary, but it will be good. And, remember, hope is the happy anticipation of something good. Your hope is back.

You thought it was gone forever, but your Savior sought you out.

The Good Shepherd

Jesus, the Good Shepherd, leaves the ninety-nine sheep who are OK for the moment to go off in search of the one who is isolated and in danger. This is not just a nice metaphor from the Bible (Matthew 18:12). It remains true today, and I know it firsthand. I have never "backslid," walking away from the Lord and my faith, but for sure I have needed saving. When I was broken, I felt lost. My own efforts did not work. I was "prone to wander," as the old hymn says. I was going off course in my thoughts, straying down the wrong path.

Most important, the Good Shepherd is the one who sought me out. It did not depend on my own efforts. He loved me even when I had backed myself into a cul-de-sac, and he still had a wonderful plan for my broken life. Although my own faith was weakened, he came looking for me with open arms. He is absolutely faithful, all of the time.

Besides being faithful, he loves us. And he is in charge of the situation—if I will let him be in charge. I have to choose to follow him. The Bible says, "Choose this day whom you will serve" (Joshua 24:15). Will I choose to serve old thought patterns or new ones? Will I choose to replace those little foxes with God's truth? Paul tells us:

Whatever things are true, whatever things are noble, whatever things are just, whatever things are pure, whatever things are lovely, whatever things are of good report, if there is any virtue and if there is anything praiseworthy—meditate on these things. (Philippians 4:8, NKJV)

If I am his and he is in charge, then I am not a victim. I can pick up my helmet of the hope of salvation and win this round of the battle. I can turn to comfort others with the comfort I have received from God (2 Corinthians 1:3–5). The very thing the devil meant for evil can be transformed into a triumph.

Triumph Over Every Trauma

We can find healing for all of our traumas in the love of our Savior. Our current difficulties tap into unhealed and unresolved traumatic events of the past. Every one of our memories carries with it a stored emotion, and a lot of these emotions are undesirable and damaging if we do not catch them, like marauding foxes, and bring them to Jesus' feet.

You walk into a room and a familiar smell triggers a memory. Suddenly you have to review the truth and ask for God's help once again. For me, this happened a lot in my bedroom at home, the same bedroom where I watched my dear wife pass from this life to the next. For five years after her death, my emotions would be stirred painfully in that room. I found it much easier to be on the road in some hotel room that held no memories for me.

I did not know what to do about it at first. But after a while I learned to take my painful memories directly to Jesus. I also had to rise up in faith and take authority over the usurper and shut down his lies. After all, Jesus is the great healer. He will heal our emotions and our minds, but we must cooperate with the healing process. Trauma and suffering walk hand in hand with each other, but I found out that I was not being forced to hold hands with them. I could march them to Jesus. He never waved a magic wand to make them disappear, but he always did something better—he transformed the suffering into faith and strength.

He will do it for you too. It is what he does best. Now you have to do your part, but I tell you the truth, he will do more than his share. He will show you which doors to shut and which doors to open. He will touch each open wound with his presence and heal it—and often he will make sure to leave enough of a scar so you will remember what he has done.

Most of all, he will restore your hope.

Changing How You Think

If you believe that Jesus is your Good Shepherd and that he is looking out for you right now, you can expect him to restore your soul, which includes your mind and your emotions. The best way to cooperate with this is to immerse yourself in his Word and allow it to be planted deep inside you. We could call it "Word grafting."

Psalm 23 is a good place to start. As many people over the centuries have discovered, it is a "psalm for living":

The LORD is my shepherd; I shall not want.

He makes me to lie down in green pastures; He leads me beside the still waters.

He restores my soul; He leads me in the paths of righteousness for His name's sake.

Yea, though I walk through the valley of the shadow of death, I will fear no evil; for You are with me; Your rod and Your staff, they comfort me.

You prepare a table before me in the presence of my enemies; You anoint my head with oil; my cup runs over.

Surely goodness and mercy shall follow me all the days of my life; and I will dwell in the house of the LORD forever. (NKJV)

He restores your soul. He gives rest—even peaceful, refreshing sleep in times of high anxiety. He helps you obtain good physical nourishment. He enables you to keep on walking, one step in front of the other. He does it because he is the Good Shepherd. He is not holding you to extraordinary expectations for performance. Victory is defined differently in different seasons of life. Sometimes, just to keep inching forward through the valley of the shadow of death is an absolute victory. Staying on your feet and following him is a victory. Paths of righteousness are not always particularly smooth.

The Good Shepherd wants to be with you and he is working overtime to seek you out. If you feel the way I did, you may not yet know whether or not you want him to find you. In the early weeks of my time of deep loss and sorrow, I was ministering in Seoul, South Korea. I was so dead on the inside, I did not know if I ever wanted to preach again in my life. But I was one of the recognized and somewhat well-known speakers, and I was expected to come up with something. Desperately, I prayed, "Oh, God, help me!" And he did.

He turned my attention to the living Word of God, both the written Word and the living Word that dwells inside me. The living Word brings resurrection power. Drawing on the resurrected life of the one who lives inside of me, I got out my notes and I picked up my Bible and I made myself walk to that podium in a packed-out auditorium with my Korean translator. I gave it everything I had and I preached on something like "Contending for Your Prophetic Promise"—even though I felt I had completely lost mine.

After that message a significant international leader told me, "James, that was the best job of preaching I have ever heard you do." What a miracle! I still felt dead, but I knew God was alive inside of me. God was at work to do his will and his great pleasure in and through me.

It confirmed what I had learned a long time before, that the life I live is not my own, but his. And he will take care of me, restore me, refresh me, and even allow me to bless others—all *because of* the unbearable suffering. That restores my soul, my faith, and my hope. As the Word explains in Lamentations (the verse I placed at the beginning of this chapter):

"The LORD is my portion," says my soul, "therefore I hope in Him!"

My soul will speak ("*says* my soul"), whether out of its despair or out of its hope and the repository of the implanted Word. That is why the apostle James wrote, "Therefore...receive with meekness the implanted word, which is able to save your souls" (James 1:21, NKJV). Our souls need saving not only from hell but from the many dark attacks that may come our way in the course of life. Surely goodness and mercy will come our way because the Lord is so faithful. He changes everything for better.

Heroine of Hope—Joan Hunter

Joan's parents, Charles and Frances Hunter, were known as the "Happy Hunters" because of their joy-filled approach to their decades-long charismatic healing ministry. But the daughter of the Happy Hunters was not too happy. She had never known her biological father, but when she was fourteen her mother married Charles and she spent the rest of her growing-up years as part of the well-known international ministry family. Joan later attended Oral Roberts University, where she met and married a young man. Together, they founded and copastored a church and had four beautiful children.

Then, after twenty years of marriage, her husband came home one day with his same-sex partner. They ran off together, abandoning Joan and the children. Divorce followed. Joan felt she had a big "D" written on her forehead. Not only did it stand for divorce, but also for disappointment, despair, debt, and a lot more—none of it happy.

The ministry of her mother and stepdad had taught her about divine healing from physical ailments. Now she reached out for herself to the God of all hope and healing and he taught her about healing for the soul. Today she has remarried and she has a reputable miraculous ministry of her own. She brings God's healing to people by asking the Holy Spirit to help identify the hidden roots of trauma and emotional disruption, and then often, along with the emotional and spiritual healing, quickly comes physical healing.

I know Joan well—she is one of my friends. And she is a heroine of hope to me because she did not let the enemy keep her down. She believes and imparts to others the truth that God has a good future in mind for each one of his children, and that hope in him is always fulfilled.

Prayer

Father, I choose to believe that I am not a victim, but that I can be victorious in Christ Jesus. I put my life into your hands. Help me to catch the little foxes that spoil the vine. Restore me from all effects of emotional trauma and abuse. I choose to believe that all things are possible. Now turn my sorrows into places where your abounding grace has the final say. For the glory of God and in Jesus' name, amen!

Finding Hope Takeaways

✦ When overwhelmed with loss, it's easy to want to shut down.

✦ To receive God's help and help from others, you must catch the foxlike thoughts that threaten to undo you.

- Watch out for downward spirals of thinking.

- Ask God to heal your memories.

- Practice "Word grafting"—immersing yourself in the Word of God so that it takes root in your heart and changes how you think and respond.

Chapter Four

METAMORPHOSIS: THE PROCESS OF CHANGE

For there is hope for a tree, if it is cut down, that it will sprout again, and that its tender shoots will not cease.

—JOB 14:7, NKJV

I was with my wife all four times she gave birth, and I learned that there is a crucial time in the final stages of labor called "transition." For the first two births, I don't remember any major problems. But with birth number three, she got stuck in the transition stage, and it was not easy. It's supposed to be a short period of time, although it is often the most painful stretch of the birth process. Michal Ann's labor was progressing right along when suddenly it stalled. She and the baby were caught there for almost an hour.

I was trying to do my cool, calm, and collected thing—soothing little washcloth on her forehead, spooning a few ice chips into her mouth, steadying encouragement ("Let's focus. C'mon, focus"). But Mrs. Together just lost it. She started screaming, "I…can't…do…this! I can't!"

I wanted to say, "I think you can, because you've done it twice before," and, "Really, it's too late to quit now." But I knew better than to make a joke. I couldn't help her and she couldn't help herself. Then the doctor had to go out of the room for a moment, and right as he came back in—bam!—he got there just in time to catch the baby.

Even though her transition got stalled, our second son was born screaming and quite healthy, and his mother's hard labor was over. In its own way, his birth happened perfectly.

Transition Time

When you find yourself in any kind of transition, especially a prolonged one, it can seem too hard to bear. You just do not think you will make it. You wish you could go back to the way things used to be before all of this pain started. The pressure can be intense, and you feel squeezed from every side—stripped, unprepared.

Yet the time of transition is taking you somewhere. Although the passage is narrow, it is taking you from a place of confinement to a place of enlargement. To keep from stalling, you need to let go of the past and allow yourself to be propelled forward.

In my time of pain and transition, I heard those exact words, repeatedly: "Let go. Let go." I could seek the Lord for words to encourage others and he would speak to me. But when I sought him for a word for myself, all I heard from the Holy Spirit was, "Let go." And I heard this for at least five years!

I had to go through an "Isaac" experience (Genesis 22); I had to be willing to lay everything on the altar. My faith was tested to the limit. I felt I hardly had anything left to let go of, and sometimes, just out of sure obedience, I did "let go."

I found out that letting go is actually healthy. Surrender is not the same as defeat; it just means relinquishment of the familiar ways. If I was going to be able to enter into the new phase of my life, I had to let go not only of unhealthy patterns but also of the old, familiar things that were good, such as my marriage. Even the good can sometimes be an enemy of the best.

I used to think that "transition" was an abnormal state, but I found out that it is completely normal. I used to think that if only I could get through a difficult season of transition, I would be home free. Well, guess what? When you get through one transition, there will be another one waiting for you. You need to be realistic about it.

In literature, a transition is the bridge between one theme or chapter and the next. It is helpful because it gives you perspective on what will be coming in the near future, and it builds on what came before. So if you feel that you may be coming to the end of a chapter of your life and you are entering into a time of transition, then that means that there is something new for you just over the horizon. And knowing that builds hope.

How you respond during a time of transition is all-important. Years ago, a wonderful mentor told me that it is not as important what happens to you as *how you respond* to what happens to you. Are you going to keep moving forward, or are you going to let your fear of the unknown hold you back? Are you going to make excuses for yourself or are you going to press through the emotional storms until you reach the other side?

Sometimes you may feel that you have been mowed down, because life as you knew it has ended. But if you pay attention, you can find hope in unlikely places. For example, the verse from Job at the beginning of this chapter seemed new to me when I found it. I do not know where that verse was hiding whenever I had read through the book of Job earlier (which had been many times), because I do not have any recollection at all of reading it: "For there is hope for a tree, if it is cut down, that it will sprout again, and that its tender shoots will not cease." I am so glad the Holy Spirit directed me to this verse, and I wish I had seen it about eight years before, because it is such a graphic portrayal of hope.

If there is hope for a tree, there can be hope for me too. As long as the roots are intact, the tree can grow anew, and so can I. This is true not only for trees that get chopped off at ground level, but also for fruit-bearing trees and vines that get pruned, sometimes drastically, in order to increase their health and yield. Right after a pruning, the tree or vine might not look too great. But remember what Jesus said: "Every branch that bears fruit He prunes, that it may bear more fruit" (John 15:2, NKJV). The trees that bear the most fruit are the ones that get pruned from top to bottom.

Transition from a Redemptive Perspective

I am trying to redeem "transition" from being a dirty word in your vocabulary. I want to help you redeem the whole process so that you will be able to find your way through a time of drastic change—with hope. I see at least eight steps in the process of transition and change:

1. **A desire for change stirs.** You may not be strongly aware of this step, although you may recognize in retrospect that you had developed a longing for something different. Sometimes you just may feel somewhat bored with your life and you want something different, something more.

2. **A new level of revelation comes.** Your desire for change spurs you to search your heart and to seek God ("What do I really want?"). Inspiration begins to come. A new concept may occur to you or an old dream may get renewed.

3. **Your present vision gets adjusted.** The new begins to replace the old, and you become willing to make changes in your life. You start to look at life through a fresh lens—you get a new perspective—and your vision is altered.

4. **Grace is received.** You position yourself humbly under the mighty hand of God, where you will be enabled to receive his grace. Recognizing that you

cannot achieve anything by your own efforts, you learn to rely on his grace.

5. **You are healed from past issues.** God's grace brings healing to any number of pertinent unresolved issues, and you begin to see some benefit in the midst of your suffering. What you are going through is turning out to be worth something, and your hope grows as a result.

6. **You grasp a new identity.** In this new season, what role does God want you to play? In relation to others, will you be a leader, a follower, a boss, an employee, a friend, a parent, or a spouse? Will you be active, or is God putting you on "pause"? Your basic identity in Christ will stay the same, but always it will be enhanced by something new. You cannot live just on yesterday's laurels; move on!

7. **You have strength to overthrow your new enemies.** With the combination of God's grace and your new identity, you will have a surge of fresh energy. Your strength will be renewed like that of an eagle (Isaiah 30:41). New challenges (enemies) will come along with your transition to a new place in life, and God will give you strength to meet them.

8. **You get a hold of your new identity.** You stride into your new land with confidence, and you secure it.

This may take a while, but you will get there if you persevere. One little step at a time is all it requires.

This whole process depends on *trust*. Are you trusting God? Or are you trusting in yourself or your circumstances or other people? Of course, the goal is to put your trust in God alone, because he uses every transition to make you more like him. That is the essence of what Paul wrote: "And we all, who with unveiled faces contemplate the Lord's glory, are being transformed into his image with ever-increasing glory, which comes from the Lord, who is the Spirit" (2 Corinthians 3:18, NIV). Believe me, becoming more like him is a wonderful thing, even a glorious thing—like being reborn!

One of the keys for moving forward through a time of transition is to get your eyes off yourself and your often-miserable circumstances. I know that can be much easier to say than actually do, but it happens by your choosing it, by God's grace. You need to follow Paul's advice and keep your eyes fixed on heaven. This means no navel-gazing. As long as my chin is on my chest, all I can contemplate is myself. But if I lift my gaze toward God, I am transformed in the process.

As the psalmist wrote, "I will lift up mine eyes unto the hills, from whence cometh my help" (Psalm 121:1, KJV). Look up! Suddenly, you are struck with his beauty, and you are amazed. "Lord, you are wonderful! You are my Redeemer. I don't always understand you, but I trust you with all my heart. I love you. I want to lift my eyes to you in worship, even in the midst of these unresolved internal conflicts. I lay them at your feet."

I think of the old chorus: "Turn your eyes upon Jesus, look full in his wonderful face, and the things of earth will grow strangely dim, in the light of his glory and grace."

Lessons Learned from a Worm

Believe it or not, the life cycle of a worm—a caterpillar—has profound lessons for us—more than you would think. At first, he's just a little thing, crawling around in the dirt all by himself. He finds something to eat and he grows bigger and bigger. This is the whole of life, as far as the worm is concerned. But changes are coming, and soon the worm will find out that he was destined for something exciting. A new identity is stirring, although at first it certainly does not look like it.

The worm feels like climbing upward, and so he does. He will never be able to articulate it, but he is beginning to feel stirrings—to fly, of all things! It's compelling. Could he have been born for this? (Could you and I have been born to soar far above the valley of despair, up into the heavenly places with Christ?)

For the worm, this is transition time, and it ain't pretty. The transition of a caterpillar is called metamorphosis, and I have been interested in this process since I was a boy growing up in tiny Cowgill, Missouri (population 259), where there is precious little to do on a hot summer day except collect bugs and caterpillars. Back then, I learned the rudiments about metamorphosis and ever since then I have remained interested in what this process involves.

Painting with broad strokes, here are the stages of what happens, in sequence:

First comes a time of normal feeding and growth. The caterpillar eats his fill of leaves or whatever, just as we eat our fill of the Word of God. As a result of this, the caterpillar grows so much that he begins to outgrow his outer skin, although inside he still has a capacity for even greater growth.

Soon a desire, an instinct to climb and explore something new, takes hold. That's all the little worm wants to do. So he crawls up and finds a spot and begins to spin a cocoon (also called a chrysalis) because, lo and behold, that something new is going to involve confinement in a tight space. It is really transition time now. As it turns out, the caterpillar spins his own "changing room," and so do we by God's grace. Hope filled and desperate, we spin dreams and ideas, visions and desires. Our time of transition can seem very demanding and confining indeed. But old limitations must pass away in order that the new may come.

Then nothing happens...or so it seems. The caterpillar is no longer visible to outsiders and he can no longer look out upon the world; he is in hiding. It is the same with us, although we may need to be jarred loose from unhealthy hiding places sometimes (I am thinking of my walk-in closet). But "he who dwells in the secret place of the Most High shall abide under the shadow of the Almighty" (Psalm 91:1, NKJV). That is always a healthy hiding place, the secret place of God.

Actually, I prefer the word *chrysalis* to the word *cocoon* because chrysalis reminds me of Christ, and as believers we are in Christ. Once the worm is in his healthy hiding place, all we can see is the chrysalis. It may seem like a resting place, a pause in the action, but there is always a lot going on as the caterpillar transforms into a new creature.

It may surprise you how this works—his body actually liquefies. Depending on the species of insect, it can take from two weeks to many months for this to take place. That old caterpillar body breaks down into undifferentiated cells that get reassembled into a new creation—something with wings that can fly! I am sure you can see the parallels to what happens to us during a time of significant transition. It can seem like a total meltdown, but then something new emerges.

You can never hurry any stage of the process. Even as a butterfly emerges from its chrysalis, it takes its time. First a little nudge here and there. A bent leg pokes out, then pulls back in. You must not "help" the butterfly get out, because the effort required for the process of its emergence builds the strength that the creature will need in order to fly. In the same way, your friends and family can never do your work for you. They can never "rescue" you from your tight place, and if they try they may unnecessarily prolong your time of transition. You are the one who must make the effort. You pray and trust and believe that God's grace is sufficient. You are the only one who can press forward and break out of your dark place and into the full light again.

Like a butterfly, you stretch out your crippled new wings.

You catch the light of the sun (the Son). You flex them. They work! And off you go, into new adventures like nothing you have ever had before. Like the worm, you have come to believe, "I was born to fly!"

Hero of Hope—Mickey Robinson

This hero of hope is one of my best friends. I remember when I first met Mickey, because I had a hard time looking at him. At nineteen years old he was a part of an elite parachuting team and was recognized as a rising star jumping with the best sky-divers in the world.

During a routine jump his life was changed forever when a fiery plane crash melted his face and mutilated his body. In the hospital Mickey had a near-death experience, visited heaven, and received a mission to bring a life-giving message of hope back to the earth. He overcame multiple terminal conditions and experienced dramatic, miraculous healings. Shortly after he recovered from the accident, he gave up skydiving for preaching.[*] But he still bears the marks of this traumatic incident.

One time I asked his wife, "I just have to know…did you marry him before his accident? Or after?"

She said, "After. I never saw the burns or the scars. I saw the man, and I loved him."

And what a man he is. He is not ashamed of his appearance

---

[*] You can read Mickey's gripping story in his book *Falling Into Heaven: A Skydiver's Gripping Account of Heaven, Healings, and Miracles.*

and he is not ashamed of the gospel. He travels the globe telling his story, and sometimes we have traveled together. Mickey is not only a warm, enjoyable man to be with, but he is a modern-day Barnabas, a premier encourager who brings hope to the hopeless everywhere he goes. Out of the fiery furnace of affliction came something far more valuable than the thrill of skydiving, and I find new hope every time I talk with him.

His life shows me what really matters. What has happened to Mickey is a perfect example of God's redemptive care and extraordinary transformation, and his life story makes mine look like a walk in the park. This dear man is a modern-day hero of hope! If God can give my friend Mickey such courage and enduring hope in the midst of the total wreckage of his life, of course he can bring hope to me—and to you too.

Prayer

Father, I believe that in Christ all things are possible! Old things do pass away and new things do come. Take my life and shape it into the next phase of purpose and destiny. Give me the grace needed for letting go of the old to embrace the process of change and to be prepared for the new. Plant desires within me that overcome the obstacles of the past. Heal me. Shape me. Make me into a person who reflects the radiance of the glory that takes me from change to change! For Jesus Christ's sake, amen.

Finding Hope Takeaways

✦ Times of great change and adjustment follow tragedies. Will you keep moving forward and press through the emotional storms, or will you make excuses for yourself and let your fear of the unknown hold you back?

✦ As you put your trust in God:

- Your perspective gets adjusted.

- You receive God's grace to let go of the past and start to look forward.

- You begin to grasp a new identity.

Chapter Five

THE DOOR
OF HOPE

*Then I will give her back her vineyards from there,
and the valley of Achor as a door of hope. And she
will sing there as in the days of her youth, as in the
day when she came up from the land of Egypt.*

—HOSEA 2:15, NASB

W hen my cancer reoccurred for the third time, it was more serious than it had been before. Having already tried most of the possible treatments the first two times, I was not really sure what kind of help I should pursue. And this time I was facing everything alone, because Michal Ann had died the year before. "Oh, God!" I cried. "I need your help so much!"

I had heard of the Cancer Treatment Centers of America and I knew that their Midwestern Regional Medical Center was in a city in Illinois called Zion. They are a privately owned institution, and I hoped that my insurance would cover their integrative cancer treatment. So I applied for acceptance—and I was turned down. It felt as though the door had gotten slammed in my face.

Naturally, I could see the scriptural significance of the name "Zion." I also knew the history of this particular Zion was saturated with healing, having been founded in 1901 by a Scotsman named John Alexander Dowie, who was a controversial evangelist and faith healer. Now it happened to be the location of this hospital I wanted so badly to be admitted into.

Dispirited and in tears, I was taking a hot shower when I burst out with a prayer: "God, I just want to go to Zion! I just want to go to Zion!" I thought of a line from Michal Ann's favorite psalm, and I recited it from memory: "How blessed is the man whose strength is in You, in whose heart are the highways to Zion!" (Psalm 84:5, NASB). Yes, I wanted to travel to Zion.

Something inside me rose up and I thought I should try again. It was as though a door of hope had appeared right in front of me. So again I phoned the number of the cancer center. Again they went through all the rigmarole about my insurance and why I could not be accepted, but I found out that the woman on the other end of the line was a believer, so I told her I thought God wanted me to be there. She said, "Well, even though it is supposed to be impossible because your insurance will not cover you and the quotas are filled, I will agree with you in prayer because you believe you have an appointment in Zion." We agreed over the phone in prayer and she said, "Now I am going to resubmit your application." That was on a Friday.

Monday, I got a phone call. A miracle had happened. I had been accepted! The treatment regimen at Zion would be extremely difficult, but I would be allowed to go through it. My youngest daughter and one of her friends came to be there with me, along with a couple of my "sons in the faith." Oh, what a relief!

Walking through Psalm 84

Because of Zion, Michal Ann's "life psalm" took on new significance for me. I was still traveling through a deep valley, but I was beginning to believe that blessings lay ahead. I read and reread each line of the psalm:

> How lovely are Your dwelling places, O LORD of hosts!
> My soul longed and even yearned for the courts of the
>   LORD;
> My heart and my flesh sing for joy to the living God.
> The bird also has found a house, and the swallow a nest
>   for herself, where she may lay her young, even Your
>   altars, O LORD of hosts, My King and my God.
> How blessed are those who dwell in Your house! They
>   are ever praising You.
> How blessed is the man whose strength is in You, in
>   whose heart are the highways to Zion!
> Passing through the valley of Baca they make it a spring;
>   the early rain also covers it with blessings.
> They go from strength to strength, every one of them
>   appears before God in Zion.
> O LORD God of hosts, hear my prayer; give ear, O God
>   of Jacob!
> Behold our shield, O God, and look upon the face of
>   Your anointed.

For a day in Your courts is better than a thousand outside.
   I would rather stand at the threshold of the house of
   my God than dwell in the tents of wickedness.
For the LORD God is a sun and shield; the LORD gives
   grace and glory; no good thing does He withhold
   from those who walk uprightly.
O LORD of hosts, how blessed is the man who trusts in
   You! (Psalm 84, NASB)

I could see that the highway to the freedom and blessing of Zion passes through (not around) the valley of Baca, which can be translated as the valley of weeping. That is how I could tell I must be right on track.

Through the Dark Valley

I have discovered that the Bible is filled with valleys. So is the natural world. In fact, come to think of it, you cannot have a mountaintop experience without at least a couple of valleys on each side. The way new mountains get raised up is by means of great cataclysms and prolonged erosion in the valleys that are left behind.

Everyone is familiar with the "valley of the shadow of death" in Psalm 23. Another significant scriptural valley is the valley of Achor. The valley of Achor is a place of trouble and distress (that is what the word *achor* means). It was named after the sinner Achan, who was stoned to death and buried in that exact valley in Joshua's time (Joshua 7:26). It appears again in the prophecies of Isaiah (Isaiah 65:10) and of Hosea (quoted at the beginning of this chapter).

Are we supposed to be afraid of these valleys? Are they death traps? Not as far as I can see. In fact, just as the shepherd prepares a bountiful table and green pastures close by the valley of the shadow of death, so does God move a door of hope into position—right in the valley of trouble. Right there, and nowhere else. The valley of trouble becomes a door of hope.

Every one of us will go through dark valleys and troubled times in our lives. After we have walked with the Lord long enough, we begin to see the truth that the place of trouble always leads to a door of hope. Always. God takes your deepest valley, your valley of Achor, and he transforms it into a door of hope. After the door of hope, Hosea says, comes joyful celebration: "She will sing there as in the days of her youth, as in the day when she came up from the land of Egypt." We will sing and celebrate as Miriam did when God had worked a miracle and delivered the Israelites from Egypt, right through the midst of the Red Sea (Exodus 15:20).

Too many of us stop in the middle. We can't even get a glimpse of the door of hope, so we sit down. I know; I've done it myself. But if you believe that the valley is only a way of passage through to the mountain heights, the only logical thing to do is get back up and keep moving again. This means that if you find yourself in a valley right now, *keep on walking.* As you walk, you will be gaining new strength so that you will be capable of climbing the mountain when you get there. And once you get high enough up on the mountainside, your perspective will change about the valley of trouble behind you. You will surely exclaim, "Why, that valley is full of flowers. Just look at them! Look at that rushing brook. Look at that green grass. I must have missed it when I was down there!" You will be so glad you kept walking.

You will echo the exultant final words of Psalm 84: "The LORD gives grace and glory; no good thing does He withhold from those who walk uprightly. O LORD of hosts, how blessed is the man who trusts in You!"

Too Many Doors

Now I have wrapped that up in a tidy, nice package, haven't I? The valley of trouble becomes a door of hope, and joy follows— one, two, three. It is a lot easier said than done though. How will you know if you are doing it right? Will you recognize the door of hope when you see it? How does it manage to stand out from all the other "doors"?

I had a dream one time in which I went through a single door, and it led into a place like a hospital or hotel—a long hallway with doors on both sides as far as I could see. The Holy Spirit spoke to me in the dream and said, "I have now brought you through a door." I said, "Yeah, OK." "And that door is going to lead you to many doors," he said.

That is often what it feels like, doesn't it? Where are you supposed to go? The time of trauma and trouble has created too many decisions for your foggy brain to handle. You are well aware of the standard advice not to make major life decisions in the midst of a troubled time, but sometimes you have to make them anyway. Even the small decisions ("should I stay home or go out?") seem difficult.

Let me assure you: if God's grace has carried you through to this point, he will not abandon you now. Reach out to him. Just lean in. He will give you more grace, lots of mercy, and (best of all) peace. You can decide between those multiple doors by means of his peace. You can ask him for guidance and peace as many times over as you need to. He is the source of all righteousness, peace, and joy (Romans 14:17), and you will be able to distinguish his peace from the false peace that may distinguish some of those doors (the false peace of escapism, for instance).

You have to understand—it is *good* to have multiple options. One of God's greatest gifts to humans is free will, and you are now presented with a chance to use yours. You can choose to follow him, or you can choose to figure it out all by yourself. You can even choose to turn away and experiment with forbidden fruit of some sort. Sometimes I think he offers us so many choices because he wants to hear from us. He wants us to consult him.

You can choose to listen for the Shepherd's clear, calm voice, or you can listen to the clamor of voices around you that want to give you advice. Years ago, Bill Bright wrote a little tract for Campus Crusade for Christ that said, "God has a wonderful plan for your life." It's true—he does have a wonderful plan for your life. The problem is, so do a lot of other people.

But the Lord will help you. God's Word will be a lamp to your feet and a light to your path (Psalm 119:105). He is perpetually in control of everything and he is more than capable of seeing you through your many decisions. God is omnipotent, omniscient, and omnipresent. He is *omni-omni!*

He will take care of you. Swamped with decisions and options, you might choose right and you might choose not so right. You might choose the right door at the right time, or you might choose it out of timing. But because God causes all things to work together for good for those who love him (Romans 8:28), he will scoop up your mistakes and miscalculations, blend them in with your successes and obedience, and come up with a blessing.

You have to lean in to God alone, as much as you possibly can. He will always see you through as long as you lean in his direction. I love this proverb: "Trust in the LORD with all your heart, and lean not on your own understanding; in all your ways acknowledge Him, and He shall direct your paths" (Proverbs 3:5–6, NKJV). Lean not on your own understanding. Lean on his. The only reason you may feel a little off-balance (besides the fact that you are probably still reeling from your time of trouble) is that when you are *leaning* you are putting yourself at some risk of falling. But you already knew that trusting faith is spelled R-I-S-K, didn't you?

You will have to lean close to him, like his beloved disciple John did, in order to hear the desires of his heart (John 13:23–25). Most likely he will tell you do something that will be quite impossible without his help. You should take that as good news, because, weakened as you are, you are already learning that you can't do much on your own.

God's Redemptive Nature

God is in the middle of redeeming you. His whole nature is to be a Redeemer. Because of his faithfulness, his patience, his loving-kindness, his mercy, and his grace, he is bringing you through that doorway labeled "Hope." God always has a good future, a plan, and a hope for you.

I used to say that he was a God of the second chance. Now I think he is much better than that. He is indeed the God of the second chance, but many of us already cashed that one in a while ago. Think about the Samaritan woman who had lived with so many different men (John 4). How many chances did she get? He is the God of amazing grace. We will never be able to count the number of chances we have gotten already or will get in the future. Now I have revised the "God of the second chance" to make it higher. He is the God of the fifty-millionth chance…at least. His mercies are surely new *every* morning (Lamentations 3:23).

The only thing we need to do is to lean into him, or as old hymn says, "trust and obey": "Trust and obey, for there's no better way to be happy in Jesus, but to trust and obey."

He Restores What Is Lost

There is a crazy story about the prophet Elisha and an iron ax head that floated on water, and the story foreshadows the events that made Jesus our Redeemer. Here is a quick review of the story:

> One day the group of prophets came to Elisha and told him, "As you can see, this place where we meet with you is too small. Let's go down to the Jordan River, where there are plenty of logs. There we can build a new place for us to meet."
>
> "All right," he told them, "go ahead."
>
> "Please come with us," someone suggested.
>
> "I will," he said. So [Elisha] went with them.
>
> When they arrived at the Jordan, they began cutting down trees. But as one of them was cutting a tree, his ax head fell into the river. "Oh, sir!" he cried. "It was a borrowed ax!"
>
> "Where did it fall?" the man of God asked. When he showed him the place, Elisha cut a stick and threw it into the water at that spot. Then the ax head floated to the surface. "Grab it," Elisha said. And the man reached out and grabbed it. (2 Kings 6:1–7, NLT)

Have you ever flown off the handle? Have you ever lost your head? Have you ever lost your cutting edge? Have you ever been defeated right in the middle of your hard work? Have you ever forgotten until the mishap occurs that what you have lost was actually borrowed? Our lives are not our own, you know.

But the remedy for the lost ax head points to the remedy for every one of our losses. We find it at the end of the story.

Elisha had the man point to the exact spot where the ax head had entered the water. (In the same way, God has us humble ourselves and honestly identify what has happened.) And then, wonder of wonders, there was hope after all! Elisha cut a stick from a tree. (The cross of Jesus is called the "tree.") He pulled back his arm and lobbed the stick right to that spot. Then a miracle occurred. The heavy ax head that had just sunk like a stone to the bottom of the river bobbed to the surface as if it were made of wood itself.

Hope! Miracles still happen. They never happen the way we think they should, but in the end we are altogether grateful. With God, our valleys of trouble yield to doorways of hope every time.

I'm grateful to report that my cancer miracle happened at Zion. I had to endure some extremely difficult and expensive treatments. I also had some powerful prayer afterward. But as I sat in a small examination room uncertain of what I would hear, my doctor matter-of-factly told me that my cancer was gone.

"What? Could you repeat that?"

"Your cancer is gone. It melted."

"You said the cancer *melted*?"

"Yes, it melted and is no longer in your body."

I left the treatment center stunned by what I had just heard. I found a small, quiet restaurant and took out my phone to share the amazing news with my four children and a few close friends. Waves of gratitude and awe washed over me each time I said, "The cancer is gone. The doctor said it melted."

Miraculously, that cancer has never come back and it is never going to come back again. I appeared before God in Zion (Psalm 84:5). I know beyond a shadow of a doubt that I made it through the valley of the shadow of death. Iron can float and cancer can melt away. I know. I am more than a survivor. I am an overcomer in Christ Jesus!

Heroine of Hope—Corrie ten Boom

Before World War II, Corrie ten Boom was a middle-aged Dutch woman who lived with her sister and widowed father. They were Christians who were active in charitable causes, and when the Nazis started persecuting the Jews in the Netherlands in 1940, the ten Boom family became part of the underground resistance. They built a secret hiding place behind the wall of a bedroom where they could hide small groups of the Jewish refugees with whom they were sharing their home secretly. They knew they were putting their own lives on the line to do so.

Four years later, in the middle of the night, the dreaded knock came at the door. The entire family was arrested (although the seven Jews who were hiding upstairs were not discovered). Their father died within days after reaching the prison, but Corrie and her sister, Betsie, were confined under horrific conditions in a series of concentration camps, ending up in the infamous Ravensbrück in Germany. They held onto their faith and shared it with the other ragged, starving women who were confined in the barracks with them.

Betsie perished after ten months of punishing abuse, but

Corrie survived. After her release, she wrote a book called *The Hiding Place,* which was turned into a movie of the same name. For the rest of her life, she traveled the world sharing one message: "There is no pit so deep that God is not deeper still." Her valley of Achor had become a door of hope, and God turned her grievous losses into glory.

He will do the same for you and me. Isn't he a wonderful Redeemer? Let your lost ax head float! Throw in the stick (a symbol of the cross of Christ). All things are possible!

Prayer

Father, though I walk through the valley, I choose to trust in you! Turn my valley of Achor into a door of hope. I believe that miracles still happen today. I believe that there is no pit so deep that your immense love cannot reach deeper. Restore me. Heal me. As I come before my Creator and Lord, turn my mourning into dancing. I believe you will guide me every step of the way, in your loving-kindness. In Jesus's amazing name, amen.

Finding Hope Takeaways

✦ God is your Redeemer—he transforms trouble into victory and he restores what was lost.

✦ Miracles still happen, although they never happen the way you envisioned.

- Don't give up too soon. Keep moving forward.

- "Trust in the LORD with all your heart, and lean not on your own understanding; in all your ways acknowledge Him, and He shall direct your paths" (Proverbs 3:5–6, NKJV).

- Look for the door of hope just ahead, and go through it.

Chapter Six

TELL YOUR HEART TO SING AGAIN

Be strong and let your heart take courage, all you who hope in the LORD.

—PSALM 31:24, NASB

I t was time for me to trade in my old PT Cruiser for something new, so I went to visit a car dealership. At the door, a gentleman met me with a smile and we talked about what types of cars I wanted to look at. Then after a while, we went into his office and sat down together. I might have said something about losing my wife to cancer; I don't really remember. But out of the blue, the car dealer said, "I am going to give you a book. The name of it is *Life Between Sundays*."

I thanked him and took it home with me. As it turns out, a local preacher named Joseph W. Walker III, who pastors one of the largest churches in the greater metropolitan Nashville area, wrote the book. I did not know him personally, but after reading his book, I decided that I wanted to meet him. He, too, had lost his wife to cancer, and I wanted to hear the rest of his story. So I had a mutual friend introduce us and I went over to his church to meet him. Guess what the name of his church is? Mt. Zion. That caught my attention, for sure.

Since his wife's death, he had worked through his deep valley of grief, written several more books, and pastored his church, which had continued to grow and flourish. He had also gotten remarried and had welcomed his first child into the world. We compared notes. He and his wife are very well educated, clearly on the growing edge in their careers and ministry. But our heart issues are the same, and we share the same Jesus. As I stood up to leave, we blessed each other.

Then he turned to me and added, "You need to know this. The heart is the most amazing organ in the entire body. It has many chambers. I will always have a special chamber in my heart for my first love, my first wife. But I was surprised when another door opened up in my heart and I saw that I had a chamber for my second wife as well. My heart is bigger than it used to be. Now it is full."

I walked out that day knowing that I had just heard a much-needed word (in Zion). I thought about what he had said about his heart, and it made me consider my own heart. I had been carrying my half-dead heart around for too long. Maybe it was time to speak life to it. I was not thinking about a new wife, but maybe I needed to get some special heart attention from the one who created it and who had kept it beating all the way through the valley of the shadow of death.

Watching Over Your Heart

I knew the Lord would be more than willing to help me. I had plenty of Scriptures to go on. For example, "The eyes of the LORD move to and fro throughout the earth that He may strongly support those whose heart is completely His" (2 Chronicles 16:9, NASB). I may have thought that my heart no longer held anything but despair, but nevertheless it was "completely his." In fact, my heart was more completely his than ever before because of how much I had been forced to rely on his love and strength and wisdom. His heart truly wanted to "strongly support" mine? How awesome to think about that!

Jesus said, "You shall love the LORD your God with all your heart, with all your soul, and with all your mind" (Matthew 22:37, NKJV). How could I rev up my heart again in order to love him wholly? In order to love God with every fiber of my being, I was going to have to figure out how to get it beating stronger than ever. I inaugurated a new goal: to end this race better than I started it. I decided that after I go home to God, I want people to say of me, "James Goll loved God and he taught other people how to love him too."

The state of my heart was crucial to the next steps I would take. I would have to guard it and look after its welfare, following the advice of the proverb: "Watch over your heart with all diligence, for from it flow the springs [issues] of life" (Proverbs 4:23, NASB). To resuscitate it fully, I would have to learn how to speak life to it.

Finding My Bearings

Any time of trials and transition is enormously hard on your heart. Even if you try to keep loving God and others as well as you used to, you just do not have much to offer. Even when things settle down a little, you remain exhausted from grieving and adjusting to your new reality. You know you are still on a journey, but you do not find it easy to get your bearings.

Finding your bearings has to become part of the journey, or you will just go in circles. You have to ask yourself some really basic questions, such as the following: "Who am I?" "What do my roots tell me about myself?" "What do I love to do?" "What brings me life?"

"Who am I?" This is easy to answer, right? Well, not when you are still reassembling your identity after a major trauma or loss. I had been married to the same person for over half my life, and my identity was wrapped up in being her husband. Now I was a grieving widower. Still, I was a father, right? Yet my kids were all leaving the nest to make marriages and families of their own. It would have been a time of major readjustment for me even without the cancer and Michal Ann's death. I was still in full-time vocational ministry. I could teach. I still prayed; I was an active intercessor. I kept thinking about it.

"What do my roots tell me about myself?" To find by bearings, I had to reevaluate my personal history. I decided to look back at my childhood and to revive some good memories. For example, I recalled the way I would help my dad, who was the treasurer of our little Methodist church for several years, count the Sunday offering after church. We would bring the offering home, and after lunch we would count the money on the kitchen table (this being the '50s, it was a turquoise-colored table in a turquoise-themed kitchen; in fact, the whole house was turquoise). My dad would pour out the offering and a lot of it was coins, because people who do not have much money tend to put quarters and dimes and nickels and even pennies in the offering plate. Before we counted the money, we would sort out every "wheat penny," buffalo nickel, and Mercury dime, because none of those coins were being issued anymore, and Dad collected them.

He would pay back the offering with newer coins, of course, and put the day's finds aside in his growing coin collection. Many years later when my father died, my sisters and I inherited his coin collection. At that point, I resumed my interest and I began to create my own collection, which includes samples of money from many of the countries I have visited in the course of my ministry. Someday I will pass on my coin collection to my own children.

Besides being a spiritual leader and father, I am a coin collector. Somehow recognizing that helps me find my bearings just a little bit more. I love to work on that collection, although I don't suppose I was born to be a coin collector. I was, however, born to sing.

Born to Sing

When I asked myself, "What do I love to do?" one of my first answers was, "I love to sing." I have been singing since at least the age of three, and in high school I won awards for singing, just like other young guys might win awards for basketball or some other sport. I didn't sing in order to win prizes; I sang because it was my life. I would go on walks down the railroad tracks and I would sing Sunday school songs and hymns from the brownish-red Cokesbury hymnal. I would sing anything I heard. I would sing with the radio. I would sing with Lawrence Welk. I would sing everywhere I went! I grew up being known as a "singer."

I kept on singing after I grew up and when I got married. (Somebody gave me a T-shirt that says, "I sing real loud.") I would sing when I was happy and I would sing when I was sad. I would sing in the shower and sing in the car. I would sing during corporate worship, and I would sing in the middle of my own sermons. It didn't matter if I was having a "bad voice or good voice" day—I would sing anyway.

But in the midst of my pain, I had not been singing much. Once I put my finger on the fact that I was *born* to sing, I figured out that one of the best keys for unlocking my poor, beat-up heart would be *telling my heart to sing again*. I would sing life back into it.

I think that is something anyone could do, even those who cannot sing a note. Even if you don't use outright singing to do it, at least you could *speak* to your heart to revive it. Tell your heart the truth. Tell your heart who is on the throne. Tell your heart about God's faithfulness and goodness and how much the Shepherd cares. Ask yourself, "What brings me life?" Look back across the years to find precious memories and helpful clues about what works for you. Read the Bible as if it was written to you personally, rereading the parts that speak most to you. To experience the hidden power of praise and singing, start with Psalms 148, 149, and 150. Tell your heart to start singing again.

I started singing again. Now I sing my pain away every day. I sing day and night. I sing in every hotel room I go into. I sing in my kitchen. I sing outside when I take a walk. I sing by myself and I sing with others. I recently sang crooner songs in a marble lobby of a five-star hotel in Taipei, Taiwan, with a classical pianist. People started coming up to take videos thinking I was an internationally famous singer. But most of the time I sing the old hymns I love.

> My hope is built on nothing less than Jesus' blood and righteousness. I dare not trust the sweetest frame, but wholly lean on Jesus' name. On Christ the solid rock I stand; all other ground is sinking sand. When he shall come with trumpet sound, oh may I then in him be found, dressed in his righteousness alone, faultless to stand before the throne.

Hidden within the lyrics and melodies, the power of praise and worship builds up my heart and orients me in the right direction. It sometimes takes a moment to overcome the feeling of being shut down, too sad and tired to breathe out a note of a song, but once I make the effort, I am so glad I am alive and held in God's capable hands.

I have a special song to sing with my life, and so do you. Not only do we need to tell our hearts to sing again, we need to hear (and learn) each other's songs. This can best be explained with a story, which, although it may be folklore, I want to share here.

Teach Me Your Song

In the northern parts of Africa there is a semi-nomadic tribe that counts the birthday of a child not from the day of birth, nor even from the day of conception, but from the day the mother first decides to have the child.

When a woman decides to have a child, she goes off and sits under a tree by herself and she listens until she can hear the song of the child who wants to come. And after she has heard the song of this child, she comes back to the man who will be the child's father, and teaches him the song. And then, when they make love to physically conceive the child, they sing the song of the child as a way to invite the child.

When she becomes pregnant, the mother teaches that child's song to the midwives and the old women of the village, so that when the child is born, the old women and the people around her sing the child's song to welcome him or her. As the child grows up, the other villagers are taught the child's song. If the child falls or gets hurt, someone picks the child up and sings that child's song to him or her. If the child does something wonderful or goes through the rites of puberty, then the people of the village sing his or her song to show honor.

In the tribe there is one other occasion when the child's song will be sung—that is when the person does something hurtful and wrong. They take the person to the center of town and the entire tribe comes and surrounds them. They sing the person's birth song, and then for two days they tell the man or woman every *good* thing he or she has ever done.

The tribe believes that every human being comes into the world as good—desiring safety, love, peace, and happiness—but sometimes in the pursuit of those things people make mistakes. The community sees misdeeds as a cry for help. They band together for the sake of their fellow tribesperson, to reconnect the person with his or her true nature and to remind the person who he or she really is, until they fully remembers the truth that had temporarily been forgotten: "I am good." They view correction for antisocial behavior not as a punishment, but as love and remembrance of identity. For when you recognize your own song, you have no desire or need to do anything that would hurt another. (That sounds, to me, like a restoration of hope.)

So a person's song is the theme of his or her life. In marriage, the husband's and wife's songs are sung together. And finally, when the person is lying in his bed, ready to die, all the villagers who know the song come and sing, for the last time, that person's song.

You may not have grown up in an African tribe that sings your song to you at crucial life transitions, but your life is always reminding you when you are in tune with yourself and when you are not. You feel good when your actions match your song, and you feel awful when they do not. When you lose your bearings, you lose your song for a time. And when you get back in touch with who you are, you rediscover your song.

It will not be enough to sing your song to yourself. Sometimes you need to sing your song for me and teach it to me. We are called to live our lives in community and we need to learn each other's songs.

As it happens, I made up songs for each of our four kids, and I used to sing to them every night when I was home at their bedtime. I remember my oldest son's the best. Here is the ending of it: "I like to dream about butterflies, I like to dream about stars in the sky, and I like to dream about you-hoo. I like to dream about you-hoo, and I like to dream about you. Bumpty-bump." Then I would tickle him and he would laugh.

I believe that God has a song for us to sing over each other, over whole families, over cities, and over nations. Sometimes when I go to a city to minister, I ask God, "What song are you singing over this city?" I ask him to tune the ear of my heart to heaven so that maybe I can hear a little bit of what heaven is singing there.

What Is God Singing Over You?

God himself is the "singing God," you know: "The LORD your God is with you, the Mighty Warrior who saves. He will take great delight in you; in his love he will no longer rebuke you, but will rejoice over you with singing" (Zephaniah 3:17, NIV).

What is God singing over you today? I can tell you that he is singing an anthem of hope. He is singing, "I love you and I have a plan for your life. I have a great future for you. I have you on my mind and in my heart. I am working everything together for you."

Hero of Hope—Danny Gokey

This next hero of hope is a singer too. He used to be a church music director in Milwaukee, Wisconsin, and now he is a professional singer in Nashville. He and I attend church and Bible study together and I have had the pleasure of getting to know him. You may have heard his name because of his music or because of his book, *Hope in Front of Me: Find Purpose in Your Darkest Moments*. A few years ago, he competed on *American Idol* (when the show was still in its prime) and he came in third place.

His *American Idol* performance took place very soon after his young wife, Sophia, had died during heart surgery. So the fact that he stayed in the running as long as he did was amazing to him. He was still in grief, and, as he puts it, "Ten months before I stood at my wife's casket and I wanted to die along with her."

Yet he refused to let his life be defined by his hope-defeating circumstances. He chose to believe that God had a bigger plan for his life. He wrote some more songs. He went on tour. He started a charitable foundation in the Nashville area that he called Sophie's Heart, which helps to meet the needs of children and families. What could have been a dead end became a detour and a new beginning. He told his heart to sing again.

"Hope" is big for Danny, and he is helping make it big with me. He did not get bitter. Even when he was emotionally, spiritually, and physically spent, he kept on trusting God. He kept following the thread of hope that connected him with the eternal life source; it was his lifeline. Hope reminded him that life exists beyond what we can see, hear, taste, smell, or touch. Hope was always just in front of him, and it still is. Danny released a new album to go alongside his book, and the title song is, of course, "Hope in Front of Me."

Three years ago, he married a beautiful young lady named Leyicet and now they have two small children. He might just be a little older than my own kids, but Danny is a hero of hope to me. We need heroes of hope in all walks of life. Are you building your own hall of heroes?

Prayer

Father, I believe that all of creation is a painting of your beauty and majesty. I believe that you sing over your creation—including me. I believe that the heart is an amazing organ and that out of it flow the springs and issues of life. My heart needs to be revived. I want to tell it to sing again. I speak life to my heart and I declare, "Hope is standing right in front of me," because you are right in front of me, even right inside my heart. For the glory of God in Jesus' name, amen.

Finding Hope Takeaways

✦ Jesus said, "You shall love the L<small>ORD</small> your God with all your heart, with all your soul, and with all your mind" (Matthew 22:37, N<small>KJV</small>). A hopeless heart cannot do this.

✦ Tell your heart what to do.

- Get your bearings by reviewing your personal history and remembering what you love to do.

- Believe that God has a hope and a future for you.

- Declare to your own heart: "Hope is standing in front of me."

Chapter Seven

LET GOD PUT A DREAM IN YOUR HEART

In hope against hope he believed, so that [Abraham] might become a father of many nations according to that which had been spoken, "so shall your descendants be."

—ROMANS 4:18, NKJV

"God gave me another dream!" seventeen-year-old Joseph exclaimed to his eleven brothers as they gathered in the early morning light before heading out to their day's tasks. "Let me tell you about it."

The brothers glowered at their youngest brother. Already they disliked him more than ever. "This egotistical kid is getting on my nerves," muttered Levi. The men shifted restlessly as Joseph told them some farfetched dream about eleven stars, along with the sun and moon, bowing down before him reverentially. *It sounds like he thinks he's not only our father's favorite son, but God's favorite too. Just last week he had that other dream about sheaves of grain bowing to him.* For the most part, the older brothers kept their resentful thoughts hidden, but they began to consider ways to shut up young Joseph for good.

And by the end of the month they had eliminated him from the family—or so they thought—his arrogance would never trouble them again. *This is what happens to self-aggrandizing dreamers,* they reflected bitterly as they drove the family's flocks home from Shechem, Reuben carrying Joseph's bloody coat to their father Jacob, along with the bad news about his apparent demise from an attack of a wild beast.

The story of the dreamer Joseph has been retold many times (you can review it by reading chapters 37–43 of the book of Genesis). The direction for Joseph's entire life was determined by God-inspired dreams. He went "from pit to pinnacle," daring to trust that God was in charge of every dream-determined decision.

Those first two dreams were God's way of showing him that someday, incredible as it might seem, he would be honored as if he were a patriarch or a pharaoh. His brothers' simmering resentment soon tried to put the lie to such pretentious-sounding predictions when they ganged up on Joseph far from home and threw him into a deep pit. Preparing a lie to tell their father about what had happened, they sold their brother as a slave to a passing caravan of merchants, who took Joseph even farther from home, to Egypt, selling him into service in Potiphar's household.

Joseph proved to be such a capable and trustworthy servant

that Potiphar promoted him to become his personal assistant. He was also too good-looking for Potiphar's wife to resist, and when the righteous young Hebrew spurned her seductive advances, she had him thrown into the dungeon with no promise of parole.

While confined in the Egyptian prison, Joseph put his dream interpretation skills to good use, making something of a reputation for himself. In due time, Pharaoh himself had a portentous dream for which he urgently needed an interpreter, and Joseph was summoned. His explicit and accurate interpretation won him not only his freedom from prison but a new, high-level assignment in the royal household. As second in command of all of Egypt, he now managed the resources of the nation of Egypt, preparing for the famine that had been predicted by Pharaoh's dream. As the crops began to fail in the seventh year and the famine ensued, Joseph was ready—Egypt would be saved.

It had been at least fifteen years since Joseph's brothers threw him into the pit near Shechem. Once the famine spread as far as Canaan, where they still lived with their father, the brothers were forced to travel to prosperous Egypt, where they had heard they could obtain food. To whom must they apply for relief? Unbeknownst to them, the Egyptian official to whom they were bowing (like sheaves of grain!) was none other than their maligned brother, Joseph. Joseph knew who they were. Was he vengeful as he looked down at the tops of their bowed heads?

No, he saw his dream being fulfilled. Fifteen long and eventful years had passed, but Joseph had not let his dream die. He couldn't. His dream had taken hold of him. Now he could see what God had intended all along. Through everything that had happened, God was going to use him to continue the legacy of his family line until more dreams could be fulfilled. Joseph said to his brothers: "As for you, you meant to harm me, but God intended it for a good purpose, so he could preserve the lives of many people, as you can see this day" (Genesis 50:20, NET).

Joseph's dreams had been planted intentionally by God, who, knowing the evil hearts of humanity, had once again made sure that malicious decisions and disastrous events would work together to bring a miraculous outcome—with blessed eternal consequences.

Let God Put Desire in Your Heart

The Jewish people are still reaping the blessings of Joseph's dreams today, and so are we, as we learn from his story how God works. And God is still giving dreams to his people, including you and me. He is still making it possible for us to move into the future with hope. The last thing he wants is for us to live in the past, sorrowing over our yesterdays.

God never lives in the past, and he wants to bring you into the future he has in mind. He wants to put his desires into your heart. He wants to give you his dreams for your life. Even if you feel that your heart has been deadened by adversity to the

LET GOD PUT A DREAM IN YOUR HEART

point that it can no longer receive a thing, be assured that your Father can fix that too. Do you remember the idea I presented in the previous chapter? God can open up another chamber in your heart—he wants to do that for you. He can increase the capacity of your heart. God is ready to resuscitate your dead heart and plant seeds of hope in it.

I have a friend who had to have quadruple bypass surgery some time ago. Three of his arteries were over 90 percent obstructed, and he could have died of a heart attack at any moment. Thanks to the surgery, his life has been preserved and extended. We call him "the man with the iron heart" because his heart used to have to beat so hard to pump blood through those obstructed arteries that it became stronger than the average heart. I see a parable here.

God knows what he's doing when he allows us to go through a major time of difficulty. Among other things, he intends to make our heart and faith much stronger. He takes us out of our dark pit of suffering so that we can proceed with the extended life he has planned for us, although we may not be able to see the whole picture until much later.

Just as my friend did not have to operate on himself, so all you need to do in order to cooperate with God is to present yourself to him. That's all. Today, this dear man, Mark Roye, carries on the ministry that my late wife started, called Compassion Acts. It makes possible another divine injection of hope, reaching across the world.

You don't have to have everything figured out ahead of

time. You don't have to get your act together to prove how worthy you are of God's attention. You only need to daringly dream the dream that he wants to give you. Present yourself to him: "Here I am, Lord." Open your heart to him, even though it seems to have been crushed by traumatic events.

Now, you might need to tell your heart that it's OK to dream again. I had to give my heart permission to have desires and longings once again. For the past few years, I have been on a very intentional journey of discovering what brings life to me—finding hope. After having traveled the world and visiting people in high places, and then spending time on the backside of the desert, I felt I needed to explore my unfulfilled dreams. I asked myself, "Do I still have wishes, hopes, and desires that I long to see transpire before the end of my life? What do I think about establishing a lineage and a legacy?"

It has taken me time to realize that I am not only fighting to stay alive just for the sake of my kids—although that is quite noble. I have made a deep internal decision that it is not enough for me to be a survivor of cancer and then just sit on the sidelines of life wearing a T-shirt that says, "Been There—Done That!" I have tilled the soil of my heart and called forth the Word of God (like Jeremiah of old) to be a hammer that will shatter any hard places that remain.

Today I am exploding with new ideas. Bucket list? Ain't got one! But I am now preparing to do a vocal music recording called *Inspiration*. I am coming back to life! I am launching other new ventures like Men on the Frontlines. The new me is even peering into men's fashion and design. I have a desire in my heart to become a Renaissance man who can make an impact on all of the cultural "mountains" with explosive kingdom of light displays.

"But," you say, "my heart is worn out." So make it a point to confess your faith in God's faithfulness. Be quick to obey when the Holy Spirit nudges you into action. Watch for signs of new life in your heart, and be ready to perceive new connections between your past, present, and future. You can change Psalm 20:4–5 into a prayer for yourself: "Lord, grant me the desires of my heart, which only you could have put there. Fulfill all of your wishes for me, so that everyone around me will sing for joy over your victory in my life. Lord of my life, hear my heartfelt prayers."

Thirty years ago, I was deeply moved by a book called *Don't Waste Your Sorrows* by Paul Billheimer, who did not go into full-time vocational ministry until he retired. This rocked my world, because he did not discover what he was created for until he was sixty-five years old. He showed me that you are never too old to discover fresh purpose and meaning in life. And he showed me what it looks like when God puts a dream into your heart. I never knew how much I would need the message of that simple book until three decades later (but God knew). Instead of wasting your sorrows, decide to follow the impossible-seeming dreams that God will start to show you. Your pain will recede as your heart gets to dream again.

Called to Do What You Cannot Perform

It's true that your God-given dreams will be impossible to perform—without him. You will need to listen for his subtle direction in order to keep pace with him.

He can equip anybody to keep in step with him: young or old, seasoned or brand-new Christian, educated or uneducated, male or female. Look what he did for Joseph's great-grandfather Abraham, who was a childless, elderly nomad when God visited him. (Nobody would have called him a "patriarch" then!) God pronounced impossible goals to Abraham, promising him countless descendants (among them, Joseph) who would make a huge difference in the future of human civilization. And old Abraham, suspending his understandable skepticism, went along with the plan. He could not have known how it would play out. He just took one step at a time, which is the same way any of us walk.

To his eternal credit, Abraham took hold of the very words that God had given him, without even having the benefit (as we do) of knowing the words of Jesus that would come after: "Man shall not live by bread alone, but by every word that proceeds from the mouth of God" (Matthew 4:4, NKJV). The word "proceeds" in the Greek is stated in an ongoing, active tense: "Man lives by every word that has proceeded, does proceed, and will proceed from the mouth of God." In other words, if you intend to follow God's directives, you must stay as close as possible to him. You will be able to listen well enough only if you're close enough.

You must cultivate a *relationship* with your Father God if you want to undertake his plan for your future. What does any good father want with his children? Good communication. There you have it. The key to moving out of your wilderness time and into something new is your relationship with God himself. He's holding the plan for your life, and he wants to help you keep up with him.

Let God Fulfill What He Has Promised

Dare to trust God both to give you a dream and to fulfill it. The Bible is clear that "the one who calls you is faithful, and he will do it" (1 Thessalonians 5:24, NIV). You have not been abandoned to your difficult circumstances. Decide to drop your crutches and follow after him. God's plans for you may well seem impossible, but you will be going forward on *his* strength and wisdom, not your own.

If you get confused or discouraged, review how God has worked in other people, especially the forerunners in the faith in the Bible. Read between the lines of their stories. Feel the heartbeat of the people who went through daunting—even terrifying—events, tenaciously hanging onto impossible-seeming promises from God. Yes, they made mistakes too (just as we do). Yet God kept taking care of them. They lost hope at times. They took matters into their own hands. They failed.

But God would not relent. A promise is a promise. When he makes up his mind, he stays the course. He engineers circumstances. He sends encouragement. He revives dreams.

He infuses hearts with hope. He also provides patience. Your dream might take a lifetime; Abraham's certainly did. Character building is an inevitable part of the process, and we should welcome it despite the fact that it may not always feel good.

Let God fulfill his particular promises for you, which will differ from his promises for somebody else. We will all be able to learn the same principles from our journeys with God, but our circumstances will not be the same. Some people around you will seem to have it so *easy*. Why must your assignment include such intense pain? Don't dwell on the disparity. Instead, help yourself to a good dose of truth from the Word of God. Psalm 37 is a good portion of Scripture to feed on during these times:

> Do not fret because of those who are evil or be envious
>   of those who do wrong;
> for like the grass they will soon wither, like green plants
>   they will soon die away.
> *Trust* in the LORD and do good; *dwell* in the land and
>   enjoy safe pasture.
> Take delight in the LORD, and he will give you the
>   desires of your heart.
> *Commit* your way to the LORD; trust in him and he will
>   do this…:
> Be still before the LORD and wait patiently.
>   (Psalm 37:1–7, NIV, emphasis added)

Steer clear of fretfulness and envy. When you discover that you are starting to get anxious and easily aggravated (or worse), remember that you belong to God. Ask him to help you understand your reactions. Place yourself in his strong hands and repent of trying to take care of your world without him. You can recover your footing with three key words from Psalm 37: Trust. Dwell. Commit.

Trust in your Lord anew today. Don't put the cart before the horse, trying so hard to believe in your expectations regarding God's promise that you pull back from believing in the faithfulness of the promiser himself. He will fulfill his promises—in his own time and way.

Dwell in God and in his provision for you. Stir up your heart to thank him for everything. He himself is your secure dwelling place, and he will always be there for you.

Commit yourself to him all over again. Confess your fears and put them aside in favor of trusting that he will see you through. The God who put the dream in your heart promises to fortify you every step of the way. Do you believe that? OK, then—that's something you can stand on!

Heroine of Hope—Jackie Pullinger

In 1966, a young British woman named Jackie Pullinger brought the hope of Christ to one of the darkest places on earth, the walled city of Kowloon in Hong Kong. On her own, without the support of a missionary society, she prayed and labored for decades, having had a dream of working for God in Hong Kong.

The walled city of Kowloon had been forsaken and ignored

by governing authorities and it had become entirely lawless. Its hovels housed thirty to sixty thousand residents (no one could take a census, so no one knew for sure), and its maze of fetid alleyways were crowded with opium dens, heroin huts, brothels, illegal gambling houses, porn theaters, and more. Days were dark in every way—the sun rarely penetrated the cracks between the rickety structures—and nights were worse, with endless vice and violence. Public services were nonexistent. Electricity had to be illegally tapped from sources outside the walls and sanitary facilities were unknown.

Jackie's failures seemed to outstrip her successes, especially at first. But by the power of the Holy Spirit, her one-woman crusade led to the conversion of untold numbers of people who had been hopeless and helpless all their lives. God had given her a dream—a vision to make an eternal positive difference in the lives of the disenfranchised—and eventually, she founded a vibrant church and a highly successful drug rehabilitation program called St. Stephen's Society, which has continued to expand to this day.

Kowloon was razed in 1993 and its former site is now a park, but as Jesus said that "the poor will always be with you." There will always be wretchedness and addiction. Jackie's work of bringing hope to the hopeless in Hong Kong and beyond goes on. Her hardships and adventures could fill a book and they have.* Jackie is another amazing modern-day heroine of hope.

---

* Notably, two titles: *Chasing the Dragon* and *Crack in the Wall.*

At an early age, Jackie let the Holy Spirit deposit a world-changing desire in her heart. Is your heart postured to receive the dream God has for you? Are you acting the dream God has already placed in your heart?

Prayer

Father, I am grateful for my past, but I need fresh pages to turn. I open my heart to you so that you can rekindle old dreams and put new ones into my heart. I want to be able to follow you into the future you have planned for me, and I need your help so that I can hear your directives and persist through hard times. I have a dream of being a source of life for those around me, and I believe that you are developing that dream more every day. I find my hope in you alone. Amen.

Finding Hope Takeaways

Chapter 7: LET GOD PUT A DREAM IN YOUR HEART

✦ To move into the future with hope, you need new dreams and goals (Psalm 37:1–7).

✦ Don't waste your sorrows; let them drive you to follow the dreams that God will show you.

- Confess your faith in God's faithfulness, and be quick to obey.

- Your pain will recede as you start to follow God's direction.

- Patiently welcome the character building that comes with the journey.

Chapter Eight

NEVER, NEVER, NEVER GIVE UP!

Return to the stronghold, O prisoners who have the hope; this very day I am declaring that I will restore double to you.

—Zechariah 9:12, NASB

It was September of 2008, and I was about to go to North Carolina to minister at Mahesh and Bonnie Chavda's church. My wife had been battling cancer for four intense years, and she was very weak. By that time, we had a full-time healthcare giver who stayed in our home and took care of her around the clock. Before I went to the airport, I went into the bedroom to sit on the edge of her hospital bed to say good-bye. She was conscious, but her condition was very poor.

"Hey Annie, I've got to go to North Carolina to be with Mahesh and Bonnie." They were our lifelong friends, and in fact it was Mahesh who had prayed prophetically that we would be able to have children when we couldn't.

With difficulty, Michal Ann responded, "Oh, good! Tell them hello for me." Then she wanted to do what she usually did, which was to bless me for my travels, but she was so feeble she needed my help to lift her hand up to put it on my head. Then off I went with her blessing.

I was going to be gone for a few days, and while I was there, I wanted to also pay a visit to Bob Jones, who was like a father figure to me. (He has since graduated to be with the Lord.) He and his wife lived close by, so I went to their house on my second day. As soon as I walked in the door, Bob said abruptly, "Well, you're graduating." I did not necessarily like hearing what I thought I was hearing, but I accepted it. He clarified: "You're going to graduate into the realm of compassion." I remembered the name of Michal Ann's ministry, Compassion Acts. We chatted about that and other things for a little while, then right before the end of my short visit Bob made another prophetic statement: "By the way, your wife has one last word to give you."

This was a Saturday afternoon. I went back to the evening meeting at the Chavda's church for the Saturday evening service. At that closing session of the conference on Saturday evening, it was Mahesh's turn to minister and I found my seat on the front row. At the beginning of worship, someone quickly walked up to me and handed me a card in a turquoise-blue envelope. It seemed like he said, "This is a word to you from your wife." I quickly opened it up. Inside was a card, and the front of it read, "'Never, never, never give up'—Winston Churchill."

It did sound like something Michal Ann would say. I put the card back into the envelope without reading the inside and turned around to thank the person who had delivered it. I wanted to say, "Who are you? How did you get this? I want to talk to you." I looked all around, but the messenger was gone. Nobody around me seemed to have seen him, before or afterward. I tucked the card away in my Bible so I could concentrate on the worship and Mahesh's message.

After I ministered at the Sunday morning service the next day, I flew home. As soon as I walked in the door, I was told that my wife had fallen into a coma while I was away and that it appeared she would not last long. So the time had come. I excused the healthcare worker so I could spend one last night in our bedroom with my Annie alone, just watching and waiting and telling her how dear she was. I knew that her spirit would be able to hear me even if her body was comatose.

At some point in the wee hours of the morning, I lay my head on her chest and told her about Bob's prophetic statement about her giving me a last word. Of course, she could not respond, so I had to believe that her last word would have to come by means of a dream or in some other way. I sang over her and prayed over her and gave her to the Lord. A few hours later, on the morning of September 15, 2008, she breathed her last.

My family's life became a whirlwind as we arranged two funerals, one in Nashville and one back in Missouri where her body was laid to rest beside her parents. I completely forgot about the card in the blue envelope.

Six weeks later, I was already traveling again. I had cancelled one scheduled international trip, but I felt I could manage this one to Seoul, South Korea. As it turned out, the

Day of Atonement happened to fall in the middle of the conference. That day is the most holy day in the Jewish calendar and has always been special to me, because often over the years the Lord has spoken to me on that day. This one was no exception. That night in the hotel I had a significant dream. In the dream, I relived that Saturday night meeting at Mahesh and Bonnie Chavda's church, but this time in slow motion. I woke up right at five in the morning while in the dream I was looking around for the person who had handed me the card. Then the clear voice of the Holy Spirit spoke to me, "I sent my angel to you to give you your wife's last word."

I thought, *That was an angel? No wonder I couldn't find the person afterward!* Then suddenly I remembered that I still had the card right inside the Bible I carry with me everywhere I go. So I jumped out of bed, full of energy (definitely unusual for me), found my Bible, and opened it up to find the blue envelope. There it was! This time, I didn't just read the Churchill quote on the front; I hurried to open the card to see what it said on the inside. The inside was even better, because it was so personal. It read: "I'll never, never, never stop cheering for you."

I understood that the Churchill quote could apply to anybody—to each of you who are reading this right now. But the inside message was even more meaningful now that my wife had become part of the "great cloud of witnesses" (Hebrews 12:1). Her last word to me and to our children was that she was going to be cheering for us from the balcony of heaven through every difficulty that would come our way.

I turned the card over to see what it might say on the back. It was just an ordinary Hallmark card, but I noticed that it had been manufactured in Kansas City, Missouri. Even that held significance for me, because that was where Michal Ann and I had lived a good part of our married life. I carefully put the card back in my Bible, which is where it has stayed ever since, so that I can reread its hope-building message as often as I want to.

Keep Your Hand to the Plow

Sometimes the words on that card kind of haunt me. Sometimes they guide me. But they always bring me hope, and I think they can bring hope to you as well. Never, never, never give up. Never give up on finding hope. Never give up on your dreams. Never give up on God. Never give up on the church. Never give up on your family. Never give up on yourself.

Even when your dreams do not come true and God seems so far away, don't ever give up. Believe that he cares for you and he intends to bring good out of everything. If you keep your hand in his, he will definitely help you "keep your hand to the plow." Do not be one of those people who look back with longing and regret. Remember what Jesus said: "No one who puts a hand to the plow and looks back is fit for service in the kingdom of God" (Luke 9:62, NIV). That is a strong statement. Sometimes it will take everything you have to carry on, but God will help you.

Think of it this way: as you keep on keeping on, know that you will always find the hope you need in *front* of you, not behind you. That reminds me of my friend Danny Gokey (chapter 6) and the title of his book and song, *Hope in Front of Me.* Always keep in mind that hope is up there somewhere in front of you, so the important thing is to commit yourself to keep looking straight ahead. With your hand on the plow, do not turn to look back over your shoulder, thinking that you might have missed something. God's heart-healing hope is what you need, not scraps from your past. You can never anticipate what kind of package your hope will come in, but I can tell you that it will not be too small. I am still investigating and unwrapping mine, still on my journey of becoming a new man.

The best will not have passed you by because the best will *never* be behind you. Yes, you may have lost some very good things, such as your health or loved ones or comfortable circumstances. But you are not supposed to spend your energy to steward the "best of the past," nor are you supposed to try to read between the lines in order to completely explain everything. Your life journey may never make sense in natural, logical terms, but you can expect it to bring you all the way to heaven with your hope-strengthened spirit intact and your heart engaged with love for the Lord Jesus Christ.

Never compare your journey with someone else's, since everyone's journey will be distinctly personal. Just keep your focus forward as clearly and steadfastly as you can. Without knowing where God is leading you, declare this truth to yourself: "I have a redemptive purpose and calling in this life! God is not finished with me yet!"

The Promise: I Will Restore

God can and will do what only God can do—he will restore. Will he restore the exact things you have lost? No. But better than that, he will restore *double* to you. This may sound like too much to swallow right now, but I am taking it straight from the Bible: "Return to the stronghold, you prisoners of hope. Even today I declare that I will restore double to you" (Zechariah 9:12, NKJV). Every time you return to the secure stronghold of hope, reaffirm God's declaration over you. It is a promise. He says, "I will restore double to *you*," "I *will* restore double to you," "I will *restore* double to you," "I will restore *double* to you." I graft this word into my soul every day.

We need to be restored, don't we? We might find ourselves in a temporary state of hopelessness. In spite of our difficult circumstances, God's Word says we are to return and become prisoners to hope. The fact is that every individual is going to be a prisoner to something or someone at all times, whether hope or despair, light or darkness. Before we first gave our lives to Jesus, we used to be prisoners of sin. We gladly traded that kind of bondage for another—we became bondservants of our Savior. As our reliance upon him grows, the more we become his joyful "prisoners." We are captives to our revelation. Today, I am a prisoner of hope and that is one prison sentence I am not planning on escaping!

We spend our entire Christian lives "working out our salvation" (Philippians 2:12)—learning to put aside our old ways of slavery as we become freely dependent upon Jesus. It is a long learning process. When extreme difficulties arise, we tend to revert to our old "masters," but such tests of our loyalty can help to reinforce our commitment to Jesus Christ.

Ultimately, we want to be prisoners of *hope,* and in order to come back to that stronghold of hope, we need to remember that God is always hopeful toward us. He is the Messiah of the Jewish people and of all people, and he says, "All the day long I have stretched out My hands to a disobedient and obstinate people" (Romans 10:21, NASB, quoting Isaiah 65:2). He does not say, "I have folded my arms. I gave them a chance and they rejected me, so I refuse to ever reach out to them again." He wants to restore you to hope and a double portion of his grace.

He encourages us to walk in the light that we have, not giving up on it even when it seems insufficient. Our present level of revelation will lead to more if we stick with it and do not disdain it. Remember what it is like for the caterpillar that is in the middle of his transition of metamorphosis (chapter 4). That is not the time to quit, is it? Your experience may not yet match your hopeful expectation, but hang on to God and it will.

There will always be things that you will not excel at, and you may think that faith and hope are just not your thing. But practice yields increase and improvement. Practice taking one step of faith at a time. Practice believing that what the Lord has said is true, even for your messed-up life. Return to him with all of your heart, soul, mind, and strength, because he alone is the source of your life and your hope.

Jailbreak Time

It is as if God has handed you a Get Out of Jail Free card, like the one in the board game *Monopoly*. If you remember that you have it, you can use that card when you need to—or you can just hang onto it and stay in jail. I wonder sometimes why we end up doing that. We stay imprisoned and immobilized in our fears or depression, unable even to pray, when the whole time we have in our pocket God's Get Out of Jail Free card, which has a cross on it. We forget, until someone reminds us, that God has sent us viable hope of freedom and that it has no expiration date.

We do not have to pay for our freedom. The Lord has done that for us, and he sets us free as many times as necessary. He is the one "who executes justice for the oppressed; who gives food to the hungry. The Lord sets the prisoners free" (Psalm 146:7, NASB).

In his hometown synagogue in Nazareth, Jesus proclaimed the words of Isaiah, and he intended for his hearers (which includes us) to take them personally:

> The Spirit of the Lord is upon Me,
> Because He has anointed Me
> To preach the gospel to the poor;
> He has sent Me to heal the brokenhearted,
> To proclaim liberty to the captives
> And recovery of sight to the blind,
> To set at liberty those who are oppressed;

To proclaim the acceptable year of the LORD.
(Luke 4:18–19, NKJV, quoting Isaiah 61:1)

When you realize that it is time to break out of an emotional and spiritual prison, you need to turn your attention to the present and to the future, which is where you will find hope. It is perfectly OK to acknowledge what happened in the past, both the laurels and the failures. But resist the temptation to try to resurrect any of it, even the good parts. You have to step out of the shadows of the past, including shadows of greatness. You may have won an Academy Award or a Nobel Peace Prize, but what does it matter for today?

What matters is how you finish the race. And you run the race one step at a time, with determination—never, never, never giving up!

Hero of Hope—Winston Churchill

I chose Sir Winston Churchill for this chapter simply because of his words on my card in its blue envelope. Winston Churchill may have had some personal character flaws, but lack of determination was not one of them. In a time of crisis, he was perfectly suited to bring hope to others, even in the bleakest of circumstances. Churchill served in a number of leadership roles for fifty years and is best known to Americans as the prime minister of England during World War II.

Churchill refused to back down from threats, and he never turned tail to run from danger. According to biographer

Stephen Mansfield, Churchill exemplified a number of what he termed "pillars of greatness." He was a thinker, a dreamer, a man of action, a giver, and more. Mansfield wrote:

> The chief lesson of Churchill's leadership is that greatness is a product of character, of matters like loyalty, sacrifice, endurance, and courage…. Perhaps if men like Churchill are indeed remembered and heard in generations to come, it will mean nothing less than the inspiration to rise above the commonplace in the service of mankind. When this inspiration fills the hearts of leaders yet unborn and they will seek to master the lessons of greatness, they will undoubtedly grow to revere the name and the life of Sir Winston Churchill.[*]

Another word for "inspiration to rise above the commonplace" is *hope*. Churchill believed that his strongest weapon was his pen, and the line I have on my card, "Never, never, never give up," is one of his most often-quoted ones. It comes from a speech he gave in 1941 that was titled "The Unrelenting Struggle." He was talking about the current war effort at the time, but his message could just as easily apply to any of us in our unrelenting struggle against hopelessness. When we are buffeted by confusing, challenging, and sometimes-violent circumstances, hopelessness becomes enemy number one.

Anyone who can rise above the smoke of the battlefield

---

[*] Stephen Mansfield, *Never Give In: The Extraordinary Character of Winston Churchill* (Nashville, Tenn.: Cumberland House, 1997), 224–225.

long enough to get a lungful of the hope-infused atmosphere of heaven will win every time. And hopefully that person will become another hero or heroine of hope, inspiring others as well.

Prayer

Father, by the grace that you alone can supply, I choose to keep my hands on the plow and not look back over my shoulder. I declare that hope is in front of me and that you will redemptively use all I have gone through for my sake and for the benefit of others. I need you to strengthen me with your faith, hope, courage, and love. Help me to keep looking forward into your eternal promises, and give me supernatural fortitude. I put my hope in you for every step I must take. Thank you and amen.

Finding Hope Takeaways

✦ Never give up on finding hope. Never give up on God, who can bring good out of anything. Never give up, even when you get disappointed.

✦ Without knowing yet where God is leading you, declare the truth to yourself: "God is not finished with me yet! I have a redemptive purpose and calling in this life!"

  • God has promised to restore to you more than you have lost (Zechariah 9:12).

  • Practice taking one step of faith at a time. Practice believing that what the Lord has said is true.

  • Turn your attention to the future, which is where you will find hope.

Chapter Nine

NO MATTER WHAT COMES, GOD IS GOOD

I pray that the eyes of your heart may be enlightened, so that you will know what is the hope of His calling, what are the riches of the glory of His inheritance in the saints, and what is the surpassing greatness of His power toward us who believe.

—EPHESIANS 1:18–19, NASB

W hile I was working on this chapter, I had what you might call a "divine appointment." One morning, the Holy Spirit interrupted my thinking with the strong sense that I should leave the house and drive over to a local commercial establishment called The Factory, where I would meet somebody. I was reluctant to stir myself; I was feeling kind of down, and it seemed as if it might be a waste of time. But the Holy Spirit was persistent, so I went out the door just the same, because I have learned that these things often prove to be from God.

The Factory is a collection of upscale shops, places to eat, and other enterprises that have been housed in a collection of refurbished warehouses. I decided to head to a café I knew, where I could order something and just sit a while. So I got my organic, freshly made juice and a little bowl filled with nuts and fruits and I sat down with it. Another customer came in, and he stopped and looked at me. "Are you, like, could you maybe be—James Goll?" I did my Clark Kent routine, because you never know who you might be talking to: "Well, sometimes," I responded. He asked if we could sit down together.

Turns out he was an old friend. We hardly recognized each other because it had been at least twenty-five years since we had last seen each other. Even though both of us had lived in the same general area for the past eighteen years, our paths had not crossed. We had actually gone together on a mission trip to Moscow all those years ago. Since we had last seen each other, both of us had gone gray (in my case, also sparse on top), and it wasn't only because of the passage of years.

We caught each other up on all that had happened in the past two decades. I told him my story in brief and then he told me his. This man was absolutely broken. He had been married when we had traveled to Russia, but afterward he had gone through a divorce, lost his job, plus a lot more. His ex-wife had just died two years ago, and now he was grappling with some new challenges. He was still a believer, but he had pretty much lost his hope. Everything seemed to keep going so very wrong in his life.

I thought of Job, so I shared with him that passage from the book of Job that I reviewed in chapter 4 of this book: "For there is hope for a tree, if it is cut down, that it will sprout again, and that its tender shoots will not cease" (Job 14:7, NKJV). I also told him to read the next two verses, although I was actually uncertain about what they said. As it turns out, those two verses are quite significant: "Though its root may grow old in the earth, and its stump may die in the ground, yet at the scent of water it will bud and bring forth branches like a plant" (Job 14:8–9, NKJV).

We were sort of like two old stumps, he and I, somewhat lifeless and seemingly uncared for. And yet the message of our always-good God is that he wants to bring life back. He can revive and restore even what appears to be cut down to its roots. At the mere scent of divine water, God's miracles can happen!

Neither of us had experienced full restoration yet, but we could have hope. By bringing us together in a "chance" meeting, God brought both of us closer to being able once again to "bud and bring forth branches like a plant." Out of his goodness, God showed us that he cares—even if we still look like a couple of weathered stumps in the ground (at a health food café, no less!).

God Is Good

That brings me to the theme of this chapter: no matter what happens in life, God is still good. He doesn't stop being good when my life falls apart (even when I happen to be at fault for some of my troubles). He doesn't stop being good when I forget he is good, or if I never understand in the first place that he is good. God is good, period.

Each one of us needs to ask the Holy Spirit to graft that truth into our souls, because otherwise we will continue to wobble in our faith. We do not yet know God anywhere near as well as he knows us, but he would like us to come closer to knowing him well. To know him is to love him and to believe that he cares.

To help myself remember this truth, I long ago adopted as one of my "life verses" the passage I placed at the beginning of this chapter. I pray it for myself on a daily basis, because I know that unless God enlightens the eyes of my heart, I will never arrive at the hope of his calling, nor will I have any comprehension of the riches of his goodness toward me and toward anyone who believes in him.

Seeing with the Eyes of Your Heart

This Scripture has been a very real guiding light for me on my journey through some dark territory. Many times I can only glimpse its light at the end of the tunnel I'm walking (or crawling) in, but it is God's light and I know it. The more I pray those verses, the more sure my steps become and the brighter the light gets.

Sometimes I have felt I was walking in a trackless wasteland, as if I have not only lost my road map but also run off the road—quite a long way back. It's as if my difficulties have almost started defining me, giving me an unwanted new (and crummy-looking) map to work from. I know, I know…the difficulties don't really alter my God-given road map. But they were so unexpected. Now I'm seeing all sorts of hidden side alleys, unforeseen obstacles, and invisible construction zones that never showed up on that old map.

This gives me all the more reason to learn to see with the eyes of my heart. When I view my life from God's perspective and let him shine his glorious light on it, all of the detours and potholes start to make sense.

The verses at the beginning of this chapter have kept me moving toward God's guiding light. Even in the midst of the worst storms, they have helped me catch sight of the light in the distance so that I can turn in the right direction. For over ten years, I prayed those verses several times a day for myself, and I still pray them at least weekly. I use those words to invite God to open the eyes of my heart.

The "eyes of my heart" give me special sight so that I can see behind the sometimes-dire things that my natural eyes show me. I want the eyes of my heart to keep functioning well even if the rest of me should get sick, because the eyes of my heart help me see the riches of the glory of God and they help me recall how good he truly is. With the eyes of my heart "enlightened," I can see with hope. When they are darkened or blindfolded—which can happen just as easily as it can with my natural eyes—I lose my way. Do you know how many things can go wrong with your natural eyes that may not render them completely blind but that impede clear vision: nearsightedness, farsightedness, cataracts, glaucoma? (I could preach a sermon about eyes, and maybe I should!)

I want the eyes of my heart—my spirit eyes—to be clearly focused and "single," as the King James Bible puts it (Luke 11:34). To paraphrase Paul's prayer for the Ephesians, "I pray that the eyes of my heart would be opened so that great light can come in and so that a picture, a vision for the future, can develop within the hope, the positive expectation of good. Amen."

The Lord highlighted this for me in a personal way some time ago. One time after my wife had died, I got up early in the morning and I was praying those verses on my bed in the bedroom, across from some glass French doors that were screened with venetian blinds. At the very moment when I was praying that my eyes would be enlightened, the rising sun pierced between the slats of the blinds and bathed my face in sunlight. I was delighted! It was a perfect picture of how this works. I still didn't know how to make my next decisions, but I knew where the light was. My confusion lifted and I just knew everything was going to be all right, because God is always good and he cares for me. He is in charge of my life and he knows what he's doing.

Take my advice—whenever you go through difficult times, pray the Bible. It works. It opens the eyes of your heart. Don't ask me how it works, but somehow two plus two equals five. With God, all things are possible (Matthew 19:26; Mark 10:27), and he easily factors in our human weaknesses. He is both sovereign and providential—and he providentially chose to give us human beings a free will, risking our likely revolt. He knows what we do to each other. He knows what the devil does to us. He's still God, and he loves us. He knows how everything will come out in the end. He takes the hands of those who ask him to guide them and he will restore to them the years that seemed to have been lost forever.

Ask Big

When you pray to God to know more about the "riches of the glory of His inheritance," you aren't just asking for an open parking space downtown. You are asking for something so big you may not be able to grasp it. Don't let the majesty and mystery of it cause you to draw back with hesitation, however. Just pray. That's what Moses did:

> Then Moses said, "Now show me your glory."
>
> And the LORD said, "I will cause all my goodness to pass in front of you, and I will proclaim my name, the LORD, in your presence. I will have mercy on whom I will have mercy, and I will have compassion on whom I will have compassion." (Exodus 33:18–19, NIV)

God had just told Moses that he knew him by name and that he had found favor, which so increased Moses's confidence in his relationship with God that he dared to ask the impossible. God reminded him that no one could see his face and live (Exodus 33:20), but Moses upheld his request anyway. He did not feel that anyone needed to ask on his behalf, and he did not ask for a vicarious experience of God's glory ("Show my brother Aaron your glory and let me just watch—in case he gets fried"). Moses asked for something that he might not survive, not because he was into extreme sports but simply because he was so buoyed by God's affirmation. His hope got translated into full faith.

I see great significance in God's response to Moses: "I will cause all my goodness to pass in front of you." In front, where his eyes could see, God's glorious *goodness* would pass. And it did. Where? Right in front of him!

I believe that we can pray for big things like that too. We can pray for displays of the goodness of God to pass in front of the eyes of our hearts. We can pray for demonstrations of the goodness of God to flood our soul and our mind. We can get excited to think of what he might do in response to our prayers. Remember, hope is a confident anticipation of good. To find hope is to discover a major aspect of God's nature—his goodness.

Looking for Goodness

The story of God's goodness passing in front of Moses is in the Old Testament. To bring it over into the New Testament, we need to look no further than Peter's description of Jesus of Nazareth:

> You know of Jesus of Nazareth, how God anointed Him with the Holy Spirit and with power, and how He went about doing good and healing all who were oppressed by the devil, for God was with Him. (Acts 10:38, NASB)

To this day, Jesus is going about doing good, although we may question that fact when something bad happens. Sometimes I have wondered if he is on vacation, or sitting regally on his throne instead of helping me here on this messed-up earth. But when I go back to the written Word of God, my misconceptions clear up. Jesus is always going about doing good, because he said that he would never leave us or forsake us (Hebrews 13:5). He sent his Holy Spirit not to touch our lives only from time to time, but to dwell within us (1 Corinthians 3:16; Romans 8:11). Right where we are, Jesus is always doing good and doing it well.

God CARES

A pastor friend, Alex Seeley of The Belonging, a local church in the Nashville area, gave me permission to use her memorable acronym: C.A.R.E.S. Each letter stands for an aspect of our seeking God's goodness for our lives:

> **C**—Cry out.
> **A**—Appeal to his nature.
> **R**—Remember what he has done in the past.
> **E**—Enlarge God over your circumstances.
> **S**—Sing.

C—Cry out. You don't have to deny the pain; it helps to cry out to God in the midst of it. You have to cry some tears in order to give God something to put into his special bottle: "You keep track of all my sorrows. You have collected all my tears in your bottle. You have recorded each one in your book" (Psalm 56:8, NLT).

I like to say it this way: Don't live a bottled-up life; give God something to bottle up.

This is the first step on the path of recovery, and you will not be able to find hope if you omit it. It is OK to cry out in absolute desperation. In fact, it is preferable to cry out in desperation. When you are at the end of your rope, you know you need God and that you cannot do enough on your own strength to make a difference. That's a perfect starting place.

It's the best way to find out for yourself that God cares about *you,* personally.

A—Appeal to his nature. Tell yourself, tell the enemy, and remind God of his divine nature—the attributes of his character—his goodness, his faithfulness, and his loving-kindness. Find particular verses in Scripture that help you recount his qualities: "Who is like You among the gods, O LORD? Who is like You, majestic in holiness, awesome in praises, working wonders!" (Exodus 15:11, NASB).

R—Remember what he has done in the past. If you can't remember a single thing that he has done for you in the past, or if you run out of ideas, simply resort to the Bible. Recite some of God's mighty deeds from both the Old and New Testaments, and let that prime the pump of your own memories. Recount how God sent the flood but preserved Noah, his family, and enough animals to repopulate the earth. Recount how Jesus Christ went about doing good—healing the blind eyes and raising the dead. Recall how he died on the cross while we were yet sinners. Then remember the time you didn't know how you were going to pay your rent but somehow God sent the money. Remember the time he made the sun shine in your

NO MATTER WHAT COMES, GOD IS GOOD

eyes through the venetian blinds to show you that he cares. Remember what he has done for you personally.

E—Enlarge God over your circumstances. All of this will help you see how big God is. Magnify him—in all senses of the word! Glorify him and praise him and make his bigness known to yourself and others. "Magnify the LORD with me! Let's praise his name together!" (Psalm 34:3, NET).

You need to get the right perspective. Your tragedy or loss is not bigger than God. He's always bigger and better than any personal (or even global) problem you can come up with.

S—Sing. With all of that buildup, you may already be singing. But in case you aren't, let me urge you to open your mouth and let out a shout of praise—even before your circumstances change for the better. Look at this exhortation:

> "Sing, O barren,
> You who have not borne!
> Break forth into singing, and cry aloud,
> You who have not labored with child!
> For more are the children of the desolate
> Than the children of the married woman," says the LORD.
> (Isaiah 54:1, NKJV, quoted in Galatians 4:27)

Your singing will change the spiritual climate around you so that authentic faith can arise. You may not feel happy, but you will be resolute. It will be a true sacrifice of praise. Something about this response changes things and shakes them up. That's what it literally did for Paul and Silas when they were in prison in Philippi (Acts 16). They were singing God's praises in the middle of the night and an earthquake came. They got set free, and their worshipful steadfastness converted the jailer and his entire household.

You might decide to go through this CARES routine daily for a while. If you do, you will find that it is good medicine for your soul. Hope will rise with the morning sun and joy won't be far behind.

Hero of Hope—Nick Vujicic

You may have heard of Nick Vujicic (VOY-*i-chich*), an amazing Australian Christian who was born without any arms or legs. His Christian parents were dismayed when he was born. Nick writes: "At first they assumed that there was no hope and no future for someone like me, that I would never live a normal or productive life."[*] But he struggled through his growing up years and God began to show him the great good that could come out of his situation.

He lives in the United States now, he's married to a beautiful woman, and they are proud parents of their own biological children. Nick wrote a book called *Life Without Limits: Inspiration for a Ridiculously Good Life,* and he likes to say, "No arms, no legs, no limits!"

Today Nick has a growing résumé and an impressive speaking itinerary all over the world. One of his primary messages is

---

[*] Nick Vujicic, *Life Without Limits: Inspiration for a Ridiculously Good Life* (Colorado Springs: Waterbrook, 2010), vii.

how to "love the perfectly imperfect you," which anybody can profit from learning how to do, even those of us who have both arms and legs.

On his list of what you need to have in order to "live without limits," Nick included "a hope so strong it cannot be diminished."* He went on to give hope an entire chapter, and he quoted Martin Luther King Jr.: "Everything that is done in the world is done by hope." Where does Nick get that kind of hope?

The same place you and I do—from God, the one who holds the future in his capable, almighty hands. A hero of hope like Nick knows that his own considerable limitations suit him perfectly to experience God's amazing goodness and the surpassing greatness of his power toward us who believe.

Lord, I am amazed at you.

Prayer

Father, I declare that no matter what comes, your character and nature remain constant, and you are good all the time. Indeed, your mercies endure forever. I cast my cares upon you because I believe that you care for me. I enter into your presence with thanksgiving and praise, and I cry out to you like Moses of old: "Show me your glory! Let your goodness pass in front of me." In Jesus Christ's great name, amen.

---

* Ibid., ix.

Finding Hope Takeaways

✦ Hope is a confident anticipation of good, and finding hope means discovering that, no matter what, God is good. He doesn't stop being good when your life falls apart or when you forget he is good. God is good, period.

✦ When you view your life from God's perspective, the detours and potholes start to make sense.

  • Ask him to enlighten the "eyes of your heart" (Ephesians 1:18–19).

  • Pray the Bible. Pray big.

  • Pray CARES: C—Cry out. A—Appeal to his nature. R—Remember what he has done in the past. E—Enlarge God over your circumstances. S—Sing.

Chapter Ten

AMBASSADORS OF HOPE

To [the Lord's people] God has chosen to make known among the Gentiles the glorious riches of this mystery, which is Christ in you, the hope of glory.

—COLOSSIANS 1:27, NIV

wish we lived in a perfect world. But we do not. I have a pastor friend named Ken Roberts whose wife was suddenly killed in a car accident. It was devastating, to say the least. Later, after much soul-searching, he remarried and moved from Ohio to Minnesota. He has allowed the Lord to bring wisdom into his life and to convert his personal tragedy into an opportunity to give comfort to others.

While pastoring in Minnesota, he was visited by a young man named Mike who had suffered something similar. Here is how Ken wrote on his blog about their conversation:

> To celebrate their one-year wedding anniversary, Mike and his wife had planned a special weekend away. Needing to earn some extra money for their upcoming trip,

Mike had worked a double shift, returned home, picked up his wife, and headed out on their time away.

As exhaustion overcame excitement, Mike fell asleep at the wheel and slammed into the rear of a semi-truck, killing his wife and unborn child. He now sat across the table from me at a local diner.

At first our conversation was awkward, but…after a few hours, I gently offered him some advice out of my own experience and brokenness…. [Ken shared how a seasoned pastor named C. Neil Strait had put it:] "Take from a man his wealth, and you hinder him; take from him his purpose, and you slow him down. But take from man his hope, and you stop him. He can go on without wealth, and even without purpose, for a while. But he will not go on without hope."[*]

Ken went on to share a quote from a former POW named David Jacobsen, who was beaten and tortured for over seventeen months. After he was released and returned to the United States, a reporter asked him, "Mr. Jacobsen, what kept you alive during the many months of extreme cruelty and the daily uncertainty of whether you would live or die?" David's immediate response was this: "Hope was the nourishment for my survival."

Again and again you hear it: *hope* is the key for endurance. And Ken is modeling what it means to be an ambassador of

---

[*] Ken Roberts, "Something Essential for Your Very Survival," posted May 14, 2014 (www.kenlroberts.com).

hope. Having discovered its primary importance, he is adding his testimony to that of so many others.

I Can Do All Things through Christ

I shared earlier that after Michal Ann died, I started to keep a personal journal so I would have a place to pour out my raw emotions and to start to feel my way toward solid ground again. After a year, I felt that the Holy Spirit wanted me to close that journal and start a new one. I thought I might name that one "The Journal of a Hopeful Man," but soon I realized I wasn't there yet. I could not live a lie, so I altered the title to "The Journey of an Adventurous Man," which felt right. I used that volume to write down my thoughts and discoveries as well as I could for the past few years. Then finally I felt I could start a journal called "The Journal of a Hopeful Man," which is still the one I write in from time to time today.

During those years I still had to preach and teach, and it was almost impossible to give of myself. I felt so dead inside. I kept combing through Scripture looking for life. And one of the places I found the most hope for myself personally was in Paul's epistle to the Philippians.

You will remember that during that first year after my wife's death, cancer came back with a vengeance and it nearly took me out. So as I was fighting not only for hope but for my very survival, Philippians 4:13 became my friend: "I can do all things through Christ who strengthens me" (NKJV). *I can do this. I might feel alone, but God is with me.*

Another verse from Philippians that I had known well for years was driven home for me in a new way as well during this time: "For I am confident of this very thing, that He who began a good work in you will perfect it until the day of Christ Jesus" (Philippians 1:6, NASB). In my debilitated state, this meant the world to me—God's work in my life was not up to me. I could depend upon his strength. I could be sure of the fact that he was not going to give up on me. *It's not up to me. I may get discouraged and confused, but God does not. He will carry me and we will cross the finish line together.*

Then for more than a whole year, this verse that Paul wrote to the Philippians sustained me:

> I have great joy in the Lord because now at last you have again expressed your concern for me. (Now I know you were concerned before but had no opportunity to do anything.) I am not saying this because I am in need, for *I have learned to be content in any circumstance.* (Philippians 4:10–11, NET, emphasis added).

"I have learned to be content in any circumstance." Those few words brought me so much of God's grace. They brought me sanity. They showed me God's mercy in the midst of frailty.

Paul's choice of words encouraged me because he did not say, "I was always perfectly content" or "I am comfortable" or even "I am content." He said, "I have *learned* to be content in any circumstance." I knew that Paul was buffeted by endless difficulties, many of them life-threatening. He was imprisoned, beaten, stoned, quarreled with, and shipwrecked. He had a feisty personality, which says to me that he was not naturally contented. But he learned. And if Paul could learn how to be content with endless hits, so can I. God will teach me too. *God is in touch with me. He knows how hard it is. I am one of his own, like Paul, and I can learn to be content too—if that means as a widower, then as a widower; if that means as married, then that means as married.* My goal was to learn to become content in whatever situation I found myself.

A fourth very special verse from Philippians spoke to my practical needs during this time as well: "And my God will supply all your needs according to His riches in glory in Christ Jesus" (Philippians 4:19, NASB). I had a lot of needs. From earlier in this book, you will remember that I was facing $300,000 of medical debt, and that I had lost over half of my financial supporters. It was an impossible situation. But with unexpected help, financial counseling, debt consolidation, and sheer diligence, all of it has now been paid off.

During that same period, my two sons and two daughters all got married—and God provided an amazing spouse for each of them. Now I have been cancer-free for over five years, and I have been released from the care of my oncologist; I no longer even need yearly scans. I am healed, and I can declare that cancer is never, ever coming back. I will never get my Michal Ann back, but I know that as I learn to content myself with being single, God will take care of me one way or the other. *God, you have supplied all my needs, and I know you will continue to supply them. I can trust you with every detail of my life.*

As I consider my "Journal of a Hopeful Man," I want more than ever to become a man of hope. I want to be able to share the good news that our God is a God of hope, our hope builder. I want to be an ambassador of hope for the sake of others, repeating the powerful truths that he has taught me: God is good all the time. All things work together for good. Something good is about to happen.

I want to participate with God in bringing hope solutions to gritty, real-life problems. This might not always be a one-on-one ambassadorship; it might reach whole cities or even nations. Not long ago I traveled to minister in the city of Detroit, which looked like a war zone, and God spoke to me twice in the same night, through dreams. In the first dream, he said, "Where there's desolation, there will be restoration." In the second, he said, "Every place where there is devastation, there will be transformation." How will God's restoration and transformation look? Better than the original, most likely. Ambassadors of hope learn to think big, as God does.

Abounding Hope

"Hope" is such a little word, but it is packed with power. Romans 15:13 announces that faith and the power of the Holy Spirit combined enable us to *abound* in hope. Hope makes us Comeback Kids, equipped for anything.

Where do we look for hope? We start with the written

Word: "For everything that was written in the past was written to teach us, so that through the endurance taught in the Scriptures and the encouragement they provide we might have hope" (Romans 15:4, NIV). As we search through both the Old Testament and the New, one "hope nugget" leads to the next.

For example, I read the words of Lamentations: "This I recall to my mind, therefore I have hope. Through the LORD's mercies we are not consumed, because His compassions fail not. They are new every morning; great is Your faithfulness" (Lamentations 3:21–23, NKJV). But when I decided to put those words into practice, I did not know how to overcome my inertia; I found that I was unable to appreciate God's provisions anew every morning.

What could I do about that? I could talk to myself. I could say, "Why, my soul, are you downcast? Why so disturbed within me? Put your hope in God, for I will yet praise him, my Savior and my God" (Psalm 43:5, NIV). "Put your hope in God"—that is an imperative statement, actually, a command to my soul. I needed to exercise myself a little. I needed to *put* my hope in God and to *put* on my helmet of hope (remember 1 Thessalonians 5:8), which will protect my thoughts and my perceptions and shield my mind from negative hope destroyers.

Once we come to Christ Jesus, we get to know hope in person, because hope is a Person: "Christ in you, the hope of glory" (Colossians 1:27, NASB). Before we knew Christ, we were "without hope and without God" (Ephesians 2:12, NIV), walking in the dark. Now we can dispel darkness wherever we find ourselves, overflowing with gratitude to God and abounding in the hope he has supplied for us. We are able to look beyond our present circumstances, because we hold the ultimate hope, what Paul calls "the blessed hope [of] the appearing of the glory of our great God and Savior, Jesus Christ" (Titus 2:13, NIV).

Sharing Hope

One of the ways I try to encourage others is in the form of sharing encouraging quotes via social media. Each morning before I get out of bed I start my day by sharing a quote that will inspire others to hang onto the hope that keeps us on track with God. Below are ten quotes I've found on the Internet and have shared on Instagram or Facebook. If you follow me, you may have seen some of these before.

- Just because you don't see a way doesn't mean God doesn't have one.
- If you can't fly—run. If you can't run—walk. If you can't walk—crawl. But by all means keep moving!
- You can't start the next chapter of your life if you keep rereading the last one.
- God loves you even when you can't find the strength to love yourself.
- God says, "Prepare yourself. I'm about to take you to another level in your life."
- The greatest test of faith is when you don't get what you want, but still you are able to say, "Thank you, Lord."

- Sorrow looks back. Worry looks around. Faith looks up!
- Blessings are headed your way!
- In the end we only regret the chances we didn't take.
- Never mistake the silence of God for the absence of God. Don't lose trust because you can't understand. He's always working.

This is just one small way I'm trying to share hope with others, encouraging them to find hope and rediscover life after tragedy. What are some ways you can be an ambassador of hope?

Heroes of Hope—Now It's Your Turn

In the previous nine chapters, I have profiled nine people from both past and present. They represent many different walks of life. Now it is your turn to be the next hero or heroine of hope. I am nominating *you* as a candidate for the latest ambassadorship of hope, and I am basing my nomination on the following passage: "So we are Christ's ambassadors; God is making his appeal through us. We speak for Christ when we plead, "Come back to God!" (2 Corinthians 5:20, NLT).

An ambassador goes to his or her appointed place, having been invested with authority to represent one nation to another. In this case you will be representing the kingdom of God to the world at large. Just as the red carpet may be rolled out for an earthly ambassador, so you step out onto the red blood of Jesus, ready to make an impact.

The world needs you. Hope solutions are in short supply. And one of the best ways to find hope is to give hope away. The world needs vibrant believers who have won their way through monumental obstacles and who can show the way of hope. Hope ambassadors know hope inside out. They breathe hope, live hope, exhibit hope, and light up their sphere of influence with hope. By the grace that God supplies, I commission you to be an ambassador of hope!

So how are you going to give hope away? Ask God to open your eyes to the many opportunities around you and then see how you can comfort those who are in any affliction with the same comfort you have received from God (see 2 Corinthians 1:3–4).

I also invite you to partner with me at Compassion Acts (www.CompassionActs.com—where small, loving demonstrations of kindness make a difference), or at Prayer Storm (www.PrayerStorm.com—where you can join kneeling Christians around the globe who are changing the world through the power of intercessory prayer). These two expressions of our ministry demonstrate how Martha (good works) and Mary (prayer) converge and complement each other, never competing. (See the back pages of this book for more information about these two opportunities.)

Out of the ash heap of my own life experience, something beautiful is being fashioned by my Creator. And guess what? He is an equal-opportunity God waiting to do something beyond your imagination.

I am out here covering my part of the territory. How about you? Will you volunteer to be the next ambassador of hope?

Prayer

Father God, by your grace I choose to take my place in the theater of life. I want to play my role in your grand drama with its many acts. I am grateful and delighted to be given another opportunity to learn about you and to sit at your feet. I believe and declare that you are good all the time and your mercies endure forever. I receive my commissioning as an ambassador of hope. Fill me with your Holy Spirit and with your heavenly perspective so that I will always represent you well. Through Jesus, your Son, amen.

Finding Hope Takeaways

✦ Now that you have hope, you know that you can do all things through Christ Jesus, who strengthens you. You are sure that God will supply all your needs (Philippians 4:13, 19).

✦ As you experience God's care, you will want to share with others what God has taught you:

- He is the source of all true hope, all true wisdom, and all true strength.

- He brings solutions to real problems.

- God is good all the time, and he works all things together for good—for you!

ABOUT THE AUTHOR

JAMES W. GOLL is the founder of Encounters Network, Prayer Storm, God Encounters Training online school and is also a Certified Life Language Trainer. He is the author of over fifty books and study guides, including *The Seer*, *Dream Language*, *Living a Supernatural Life*, and *Passionate Pursuit*. He is the father of four married adults and has a growing number of grandchildren. James continues to make Franklin, Tennessee, his home.

www.encountersnetwork.com

Facebook: jamesgollpage

Instagram: jamesgoll

Twitter: @jamesgoll

YouTube: EncountersNetwork

PO Box 1653, Franklin, TN 37065
Email: info@encountersnetwork.com
Phone: 615-599-5552
Toll Free: 1-877-200-1604

The Hour That Changes The World

Releasing the Global Moravian Lampstand

> *"Fire shall be kept Burning continually on the altar; it is not to go out."*
> **-LEVITICUS 6:13**

The Vision of PrayerStorm is to restore and release the Moravian model of the watch of the Lord into homes and prayer rooms around the world.

Web based teaching, prayer bulletins, and resources are utilized to facilitate round-the-clock worship and prayer to win for the Lord the rewards of His suffering!

Hourly worship and prayer around the world will be maintained with four primary emphases:

REVIVAL IN THE CHURCH

PRAYER FOR ISRAEL

WORLD'S GREATEST YOUTH AWAKENING

CRISIS INTERVENTION THROUGH INTERCESSION

GOVERNMENTAL INTERCESSION

Find out More at:
PrayerStorm.com

Compassion Acts was founded by Michal Ann Goll in 2004 as a ministry and humanitarian aid organization to provide help for those in need. Even though she is no longer with us today, we still carry on the heart and soul of Compassion Acts in her stead.

Today, Compassion Acts operates in a pursuit of justice, disaster relief and humanitarian aid work in response to Michal Ann's personal charge found in her last will and testament.

CA EFFORTS AROUND THE WORLD

Mission Projects -
sending resources and volunteers to help meet specific needs

Emergency Relief -
responding to natural disasters through rice shipments and humanitarian aid

Project Dreamers Park -
building playgrounds and community centers to inspire children to dream

First Nations in America -
serving Native Americans by providing food, health supplies and education

Want to Get Involved? Find out More at:
CAMPASSIONACTS.COM

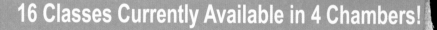